CHURCH
IN
FRENZY

CHURCH IN FRENZY

The Reverend Canon
William V. Rauscher

ST. MARTIN'S PRESS / NEW YORK

Design by Manuela Paul

Library of Congress Cataloging in Publication Data

Rauscher, William V.

  Church in frenzy.

  1. Christianity—United States. 2. United States—
Church history—20th century. I. Title.
BR526.R37   237'.082   80-23562
ISBN 0-312-13478-9

To
The faithful members and friends
of
Christ Church
Woodbury

TABLE OF CONTENTS

FOREWORD

by
The Reverend Canon Robert J. Lewis
Rector
Church of the Incarnation, New York City

Canon Rauscher has been active on many spiritual frontiers in the course of his ministry and therefore has not always enjoyed ecclesiastical bliss among the clerical and lay hierarchy of the church. When he first told me about this book I thought it should not be written. It would be easy to say that he is merely another muckraker or that he has accumulated incidents that do not tell the real story.

I can hear the voices of some who would say of this book, "The church has always been in frenzy even since apostolic days." "The church has always grown and prospered as a result of the divine tension between what we call the conservative and the liberal." "This is the Holy Spirit in action."

After reading this book carefully I am convinced that the author has done a service to the church by indicating what are specific trends, and they are not likely to change in the near future. Whatever happened to religion?

This book tells of events that have shaped people's opinions of today's organized religion in America and elsewhere. If there is hope for the church then those in positions of authority and decision making must reassess the direction and path in which the church has been led. We ask the question, "Is the present state of religion a result of the Holy Spirit or human manipulation?"

We have known the world to be in frenzy ever since man has recorded history, but for the Church of God to be in frenzy deliberately perpetrated by men and women within the household of faith is an awesome and dangerous course. To quote the psalmist, "He that troubles his own house shall inherit the wind."

We know that the church has been a barometer of society. It reflects and originates trends, it deals with excesses both in the dilemma of its dignity as well as in its accessibility. Yes, the church has always been in frenzy; however, the flamboyant opportunism of the present is new and not historical. The traditional fermentation of the Spirit is one thing, but the competing in the marketplace with faddist tricks designed to attract attention and to bring into the evangel of the church the current promotional techniques of the bizarre is in no way reflective of the *mysterium tremendum* we know to be Divine Providence.

Twenty-five years ago, preparing for the priesthood in the Episcopal Church, I was taught that the Episcopal Church was part of what was known as the worldwide Anglican Communion. Since that time there has been an obvious breakdown in the solidarity of attitude and direction among its many member branches. The Lambeth Conference of Anglican Bishops every ten years in England may well be abandoned within our own lifetime. The "unity of faith" under the guise of pan-ecumenism is becoming more and more a parochial circus.

The author speaks from the busy world of parish life and not from the platform of some group or lobbying organization within the churches. Here is a down-to-earth, on-the-scene sharing of a local parish priest amidst all the obligations of a pastoral ministry. Day-to-day life in most parishes is a personal sacrifice in Christ's name. It is a complicated milieu of conducting services both public and private, counseling, administration, parish calling, meetings, pastoral encounters on the street and in the shop, preparation of talks, sermons and most often a morning-to-evening routine with an expenditure of physical and emotional energy in what can be called a juggling operation. It was while these things were taking place that Canon Rauscher observed the many events and happenings that were to shape the intent of this book. There is no superior attitude here, but many times a good laugh at how human religion can be yet how divine in essence. The book is also a prophetic note for the future. The author is really calling for good common sense and a true mystical view of what may be the real meaning of religion at its best.

Times have changed, but as Rector of a Madison Avenue Church, I can attest to the fact that people, even in the stone jungle of Manhattan, still have the basic need for a sense of something spiritual in worship which many churches are not providing. The Holy Mysteries still call them in their deepest need. How the church answers that mysterious need is the real problem for religion.

When the late President of Union Theological Seminary, Henry Pitney Van Dusen, entered into a suicide agreement with his wife in January of 1975 and she died while he lived because of failure to digest the pills, it was a strong hint of how far such subjects as "situation ethics" had taken over religion. When I saw a large banner in procession in an Episcopal Church which read, "The Episcopal Church—Love It Or Leave It," I knew that longtime members who espoused a traditional view of the Holy Communion or did not approve of women priests were now considered the dissidents. When I realized that clergy were really serious about forming unions and possibly going on strike even though they depend on offerings, I knew that commitment to Christian vocation was suffering. When I thought about Archbishop Oscar Romero of San Salvador shot to death as he raised the chalice during mass, I realized the further breakdown of the sacred to the power of the secular. When I read *Give Me That Prime Time Religion,* by Jerry Sholes, on the impact and internal workings of the Oral Roberts T.V. Church, I realized how beyond belief was the understanding of the local church in respect to the financial structure of the emerging Cathode Church, as *Time* called it. When a Moonie told me that she compared the recognized church in its ineffectiveness to the appeal of Mr. Moon she had to recognize the truth, I realized the hold contemporary cults were having on our youth. I could go on.

Where is hope in all of this? It lies in the future. Read as apocalypse the author's chapter—Future Church. It is in the subtle unfolding guidance of the Holy Spirit who can easily be diverted by what appears to be relevant in contemporary society or ignored by our "instant everything" generation, including the absence of adolescence in the human maturation process, that we truly hail the time appointed to put things right, to alter or change things for the better even if abandoning what was newly adopted as correct. Hope lies in a behavioral pattern that is becoming to any great church with an awesome history and a mystical heritage.

With the thought of Teilhard de Chardin, as we approach the 21st Christian Century, we look to a Cosmic Christ and a concept of spiritual evolution and a final arrival of all truth in that Omega Point—the ultimate goal to which all good and bad is moving. To all of this, Canon Rauscher addresses his inquiries and observations. This book is a unique contribution and one which raises the age-old question of the psalmist, "For if the foundations be cast down, what can the righteous do?"

CHURCH IN FRENZY

INTRODUCTION

As you begin this journey through the maze of contemporary religion in America, let me say that what is depicted here is a mirror view, a reflection, a series of shadows that stare the church in the face as she looks at herself today. Standing in those shadows, however, are countless faithful parishioners everywhere who want very much to be led into the light. I hope that this book may be a beacon for some who have waited for so long. They will be the first to understand that the insights and events recounted here are indications of weakness in the fabric of man's search for God. They will understand that the real changes needed by the church in our day are to be seen in the example set by those who faithfully represent the church. And they will know that the plea made by this book is not for reformation but restoration.

This book is not to be considered an apologia for the church. It is not a heavy scholarly dissertation designed to carry forward an esoteric theological argument; nor is it meant to defame or to mock or to embarrass anyone. My readers are simply asked to accept honest reporting in order that they, as intelligent individuals, may view the whole picture of the church today in a comprehensive way.

I have tried to bring to this account certain insights that have come my way through the years as an experienced parish priest. I want to go on record as a man who believes in God and in the goodness of those who seek him within the structure of what we have come to know as "organized" religion. Some things the reader is certain to disagree with, just as he or she is sure to agree heartily with other parts of the picture I draw. Even so, I believe that there are great and grand traditions that have been and are being maligned and distorted in today's religious scene.

The church is, indeed, in frenzy today. If we are to live our Christian faith in the midst of that frenzy and, in fact, minister to it in the name of our Lord, then we must first understand it.

How have all these things that we shall discuss come to pass? In the course of this volume, I hope to answer that question. But, of course, it is now nearly impossible to enumerate all of the events and the people who have brought about and are a major part of this frenzy. Twelve years ago, women priests were anathema to the church at large. Twelve years ago, Garner Ted Armstrong's church was just a small, little-known group; now it is a wealthy enterprise—even if it does seem to be in some difficulty. Twelve years ago, the Fundamentalists were with us, but they seemed to be a dying force. Now they are an outspoken religious and political force in the "Electronic Church." Twelve years ago, the Charismatics were a trickle in the stream of religion; now they are emerging as a separate church.

In a book such as this, the reader deserves to know more about the author than is the case with most other books. So let me say first of all that what is reported in this book in no way affects my own committed faith in the fact that man must have a path, a road to God. But he must be led in the right way—or he will perish in even stranger ways. I stand firm in the apostolic tradition. I affirm my faith in Jesus Christ and in God as my Heavenly Father. I believe that it is one's faith in Jesus Christ that will save him, regardless of the church to which he may belong. That is one of the things I wish to show in this book: How one is led by the example and direction of a church may well determine his destiny. What is the church in our day? Who leads it? Who are its faithful members?

Is there hope for the church in our day? Yes. I do not doubt for a single moment the power of the Holy Spirit to lead us through the present frenzy to a better day and a better church. I confess that it seems to me that we are dangerously near what pilots call "the point of no return." It is late and growing later. But it is not too late for Christian men and women everywhere to ponder very seriously the profound meaning of Saint Augustine's words:

The new in the old concealed,
The old in the new revealed.

CHAPTER ONE

WOULD YOU BELIEVE?

Strange things are happening in religion. The staid behavioral patterns of yesteryear have emerged in our day as uncontrolled, informal, undisciplined, ultraliberal, and often bizarre practices. A longtime parishioner who was very devoted to every project in her church in California summed it up by saying, "I don't attend anymore because the church has just gone nuts!"

Zany antics are taking place not only in the American church, they are also to be found all around the world. Distraught by "the existence of insurmountable differences in the field of religion and the shaping of the Christian way of life in the parish," a clergyman in Falkenstein, East Germany, ignited himself from the altar candles and burst into a human inferno before three hundred horrified parishioners. Was it a symbol of the once sensible going up in flames? That forty-one-year-old Evangelical pastor, riddled with tensions, had served ten years in Falkenstein before he prepared himself as a sacrifice with a flammable fluid in his sacristy.

Yes. These are hectic times in the modern church. Religion, which is supposed to make people healthy, can also make them very sick. Under the guise of godliness, clergy can and do shape the lives of countless thousands of people. And there is one power that the clergy has that transcends all others: the power of the pulpit. Has that power been misused or misdirected? Today, in an effort to rescue and update the churches, every conceivable approach to worship is being tried. The fear of boredom with the church is a threat to many clergymen. So they design and implement what they feel will excite and stimulate people in a new and always experimental approach to God. Such a fear of boredom reached a high point in California recently when a parishioner was charged with physically attacking a priest during mass. The man was bored with the sermon. "God made me do it," he told the police.

Not only are clergy looking for new ways to present God and thus rescue their dying congregations and ebbing treasuries, but many have turned to secular interests, social reform movements, and political causes. Rev. L. A. Rogione, O.S.A., stated in a review of the book *Pagans in the Pulpit,* by Robert S. Wheeler, that "the obsession with secular reform among some clergymen is nothing less than apostasy from both the Jewish and the Christian faiths." He went on to say that "a segment of the clergy seems to have an identity crisis . . . they grope in the midst of philosophical doubt, theological uncertainty, and moral ambivalence." The recent visit of Pope John Paul II to the United States affirmed his conviction that a message was needed to all priests urging them to reaffirm within themselves a new dedication to their calling as priests.

It is a false notion that religion is on the upswing. Bad publicity, misbehavior of clergy, loss of faith in church structure, and engrossing worldliness have all contributed to an overall decline in church membership. The monthly Princeton Religion Research Center's *Emerging Trends Newsletter* reported in February 1979 that an overall gradual decline even in church attendance has been taking place since 1958.

And the Gallup Poll reports regularly that its statistics are similar. Most clergy will say, in defense, that attendance is not growing by leaps and bounds, and that the list of members does not correspond to actual attendance. Moreover, churches usually carry a large fringe group that is paid for by regular members. It is these fringe members who use the church for baptisms, weddings, and funerals.

The work of George Gallup showed that youth today are "turned off" by organized religion. They report that "bingo, bazaars, and bad sermons" are what church is all about. They believe that a person can be a good Christian and not ever attend church. (We shall have more to say about this in the chapter on the Eastern religions.) Gallup also sees a moral crisis in the "shape of the 1980s." Such things as cheating, little or no ethical standards in the professions, violence, crime, and general lawlessness are shaping the future. Along with these trends there is a growing undercurrent of spiritual restlessness. Young people, in their natural zeal, have turned to the more evangelical movements, and the mainline churches have imitated, in many ways, these very extreme protestant antics at which they once looked down their noses.[1]

What the public reads about churches and clergy shapes its view of what it wishes to identify with. Those in positions of regional or national authority in various denominations fail to take into account that, even though the headquarters programs are functioning comfortably, the public is often distraught by what it reads of the church and how it affects the faithful. A cathedral dean wrote in a newsletter that he was saddened by what he felt was misleading in the local and national press reports. What he failed to say was whether or not the many reports in the press about church gymnastics were true. There is often a note of humor in church activity and in the actions of those who stand in the pulpit. There is also a note of sadness in seeing how far afield the faithful can be led.

The example set by the Women's Triennial of the Episcopal Church in 1969 in condoning abortion is second only to the attempt of the bishop of Winchester in England who failed to get a prayer into the new worship book. The prayer was for use after an abortion: "Heavenly Father, you are the Giver of Life and you share with us the care of the life that is given. Into your hands we commit in trust the developing life that we have cut short. Look in kindly judgment on the decision that we have made and assure us in all our uncertainty that your love for us can never change. Amen." Another example of how far afield some can go is the effort by some clergy to conduct gay marriages in which the phrase "so long as we both shall love" provides the proper escape clause.

The state of marriage is further complicated by the increased use of a new church law, especially in the Episcopal church, of the marriage of divorced persons. Supposedly for those known by the clergy and approved by the bishop, it is rarely followed with discretion except by a more conservative clergy. People who are sincere are not encouraged by the church when they read that Rex Harrison, who was married six times and divorced five times, (a wife died) and married for the seventh time, received the blessing of the church at the Little Church Around the Corner in New York City. Although the service was conducted by the rector with the permission of the bishop, it poses problems for many Episcopal clergymen who are trying to exercise care, and for sincere parishioners who have been refused marriage. Nor is it helpful to local churches when they deal with such aftereffects as the seventh marriage of Elizabeth Taylor Hilton Wilding Todd Fisher Burton Warner by an Episcopal rector in Middleburg, Virginia. Is such a wedding "signifying unto us the mystical union that is betwixt Christ and his Church . . . and therefore not to be entered into unadvisedly or lightly?" A bishop gave his permission for the marriage based on the pastoral concern of the rector.

In another case, a priest told me how he had counseled a

divorced couple seeking marriage in the church. He wanted his bishop to have the papers before he went on vacation. The bishop's secretary simply told him to send them in because the bishop had already left. He had pre-signed the permissions and so she would send him one at once. The illusion of the bishop making any pastoral judgment wasn't really necessary. Canon law in most minds has become merely guidelines or, at best, canonical discretion.

The manner in which weddings are conducted today can be very traditional or very extreme. It all depends on the pastor. One girl may want her neighbor to sing "Indian Love Call," another may want to come up the aisle to the music of "How Do You Solve a Problem Like Maria?" Couples may want to be married outdoors, indoors, on a stage, in a horse barn, or in a balloon. A magician friend of mine started a stage illusion with all his friends in the audience—and then vanished. He immediately reappeared at the back of the theater to walk down the aisle with his bride while his fellow magicians held aloft large wands under which the couple walked. If a couple can think it up, it can happen. Today's "Christian" marriage can contain anything from a reading of Gibran to a poem by Timothy Leary. A new Baptist service book has updated the wedding vows by adding, "I will love you when it is easy and when it is difficult. I will love you when I love you and when I hate you."

One of the most unusual weddings reported in the press recently was a go-go wedding in which the bride wore white pasties, white G-string, white cape, white stockings, and white shoes. The four bridesmaids also wore G-strings. After the wedding, performed by the Runnemede, New Jersey, mayor, the bride did her nuptial go-go. These unusual services, if they can be termed services, are not unique to the non-mainline churches.

In Maryland, on an Ash Wednesday, to symbolize repentance for Vietnam and a dozen other types of injustices, the ashes applied to the foreheads of about a hundred men and women consisted of human blood, olive oil, tax forms, and a draft card. A slight variation from the usual burning of blessed palms of the previous Lent. Vestments at Grace Cathedral in San Francisco are now spangled with flowers, butterflies, and red and yellow colors, and are as mod as possible. One bishop's consecration was akin to a carnival. The *National Laymen's Digest* reported it "replete with minstrels, noisemakers, flashes of 'worldly sense of life' on four suspended screens, clowns doing pratfalls and 2400 cans of beer given away free."

The consecration of the bishop of Utah was similarly reported as taking place with confetti, firecrackers, and balloons, and was described as an ecclesiastical hootenanny.

To top that encounter, one had only to read reports of some of the services held at various meetings of clergy, especially the one at the general convention of the Episcopal Church in 1969. This was called the "Clown Mass" in which the celebrant was dressed as a clown in full makeup. During the communion each person receiving was marked with clown paint before receiving the Sacrament.

Services have also been held such as the one at the general convention of 1970 in which bottles of "cold duck" were used. During the service people smoked, talked, and finally joined in a snake dance to the tune of "Let the Sunshine In." At one of the seminaries, a student told me that the seminarians prepared for the Eucharist by smoking marijuana. This gave them the full effect of "communion," he said. It was their own preparation for a unique service of their own devising. Arrests of clergy for possession of marijuana have occurred. A Nigerian priest and two others were apprehended at Rome's Leonardo da Vinci Airport with seventeen pounds of marijuana in their baggage in February 1980.

Music, once sacred, has also taken on a secular note in numerous services. In historic Trinity Church, on Wall Street, a synthesizer adds to the theme of what one priest called "a Star Trek effect." He whispered to his friend during a Trinity Institute service in January, 1980, "This is a close encounter of the liturgical kind." For some time the top tune on the Roman Catholic Sunday service hit parade was "Eat My Flesh, Drink My Blood, Allelu, Allelu, Allelu." Other religious groups used it and finally everyone got sick of it. Songs range from rock to Bach, including handclapping and toe tapping. A former choir member of a large and once thriving church said to me, "If I hear one more rendition of 'Let Us Break Bread Together in the Lord' or 'You Light Up My Life,' I'll begin to think we are an after-dinner theatre. A Holy Ghost entertainment center." A religious secularist (yes, that's what he said he was) put it more bluntly, "My God, when the hell are they going to stop this shit?" In the meantime the beloved Jimmy Durante was buried from the Roman Catholic church while the organist played, "Inka Dinka Doo" and "Give My Regards to Broadway."

One priest's plan for Easter included the night before vigil but with his special touch. He told me, "I plan to give everyone a bell when they enter, a real bell like a school bell, jingle bells or a cow bell. During the Gloria in Excelsis Deo they will all ring their bells in total darkness. In the dark, the altar guild will rush in with potted flowers by the dozens. When the lights come on it will be Easter. Now, it may be confusing but that's what Easter was—Holy Confusion!"

Another priest's plan for the usual Palm Sunday was to advertise for people so they could join the Palm Sunday Parade. The church bulletin read, "It will be fun." He then backed it up by quoting from the anthem, "O'er all the way with palms and blossoms gay." Since when is the theme of Palm Sunday fun?

Attending a clergy meeting, I observed a Eucharist in the church basement using a folding table as the altar because it was more "intimate" than the formal surroundings upstairs. A large champagne glass was used in place of the chalice and a large loaf of bread accompanied it. The order of service was mimeographed. Some clergy whispered, "Salvation by mimeograph." The pieces of bread that were distributed were large enough to make sandwiches; the people were actually munching great hunks of bread. And when I left the church I watched the assistant out in the backyard distributing the leftover "consecrated" bread—to the birds. The psychedelic worship service is still with us. As an experiment in liturgy, one church combined electronic music, strobe lights, go-go girls, and poetry readings. It was billed as a church service and a "trip without acid." Guitar, organ, and drums are the usual instruments for such services. In the midst of this particular nightclub act, some one hundred people danced in the aisles of the church. The dancing sermon is another act that appears in some churches. One such sermon was "performed" at the Cathedral of Saint John the Divine in New York City during Sunday worship in an attempt to "preach" Psalm 45.

During the wild 1960s, a special service in Grace Cathedral, San Francisco, resulted in a wrestling match between the dean and a projectionist who sat on the high altar smoking a cigar. There were almost three thousand people present. The projectionist on the altar gave the dean "the finger" as he beckoned him off the sacred place. On seeing the sign of the finger, the dean leaped on the projectionist and together they rolled to the floor. In the midst of all this, banners, bells, pictures, lights and flowers, a blues band, and the organ music surrounded the "worshipers."

The loss of dignity in many of these "events" caused one church writer, the controversial but incisive Lester Kinsolving, to say that such services have "all the dignity and solemnity of the center aisle at the Democratic Convention or the center ring at Ringling Brothers Circus."

When Francis B. Sayre was dean of National Cathedral in Washington, this same kind of circus-type approach to liturgy was planned by then-Canon Jeffrey Cave. The good canon intended to have "six clowns and a unicycle act from the Ringling Circus" take part in an Easter service. Fortunately, the clowns refused the invitation. Canon Cave is gone from the cathedral and there is no evidence that he ever joined the greatest show on earth.

National Cathedral, once the recipient of financial support from those convinced by its stately approach to the liturgy of the church, has now lost many of its supporters. One longtime communicant regards the changes there as the most drastic she has seen. She says, "The deep sense of the sacred has given way to a broad and secular humanism." People of deep devotion are not willing to go along with everything from folk masses to invocations to "The Mother, the Daughter, and the Holy Spirit."

One of the most neurotic of such services was reported in *The New York Times,* January 27, 1969. At Saint Clement's Episcopal Church in New York City, the worshipers were blindfolded. Barefooted, they were led upstairs and tossed bodily into the air. They crawled on their hands and knees and were assaulted by unseen voices and colored lights. The culmination of this strange liturgy was the final arrival of the "pilgrim" to a bathroom where his blindfold was removed and a "smiling individual with toilet paper draped around his neck flushed his sins away in a symbolic declaration of absolution." It all ended in the sacristy where the pilgrim was administered communion. One worshiper said of this experience, "It was a bit weird."

Gaining attention through exotic means or bold gestures is one way that today's clergy think they can keep the people coming, especially the youth. A Woodbury, New Jersey, Baptist clergyman told me how he actually stood on his head for his youth during a Sunday service. Recently, another Baptist clergyman was shown on television playing a guitar with his toes. "God has given me this gift," he said, "and it brings me closer to the young people." A Drexel Hill, Pennsylvania, Methodist minister dressed in a costume with a clown face to help his congregation concentrate. An ad in a Vineland, New Jersey, paper once announced that if the pastor of a certain church had 100 people attend Sunday school, he would eat his lunch in a tree. Several weeks later, the ad announced that "If we have 150 people in Sunday school, the pastor will let the church school superintendent hit him in the face with a cream pie." One can only imagine what he might do if 1000 people turned up.

This is surely the age of the gimmick ministry. It is an age when clergy will build sixteen million-dollar Crystal Cathedrals in California or, in Frostburg, Maryland, a building which is a full-size replica of Noah's Ark at a cost of $1 million. The pastor of the Frostburg Church of the Brethren believes that this is a new way of saying that we are saving people. He also believes that the end is coming.

Clergy are desperate to keep their congregations and to keep them growing, since loss of members is bad for the reputation of a clergyman. In Garrytown, Iowa, the pastor of Saint Patrick's Roman Catholic Church was so annoyed at people leaving his church, especially during communion, that he had electric locks installed on the sanctuary doors . . . locks that he could operate from the altar. When people started to leave, he simply locked them in. (The locks were later removed by order of state officials.)

Everything from new norms of worship to "Joggers' Masses" and Saturday Night Church (so that Sunday can be reserved for golf) is seen on the current bulletin boards of churches of all denominations. Gimmickry in worship can, and does, include tambourines, dialogue sermons, oriental concentration sessions, and therapy encounter groups of the "touchie-feelie" kind. All around the world of the church this kind of activity has masqueraded as renewal. But sometimes it backfires. At London's Saint Paul's Cathedral, the dean planned to have a Holy Communion service with songs from the musical *Hair.* The musical would be the focus of a Eucharist in which the choir would praise drugs and nudity. All hell broke loose. Hundreds of demonstrators crowded the steps one night to protest. They did not like it at all. But the service was held.

The use of gimmickry in worship was well in evidence at Grace Cathedral in San Francisco many times during the 1970s. During one twenty-four-hour vigil, poet Allen Ginsberg wore a deer mask while two senators were named godfathers of the tule elk and the California brown bear. The vigil was held by the Living Creatures Foundation; a letter addressed to the dean called the service "a profane employment of this sacred house of worship . . . a betrayal of trust of a great number of people who in the past have sacrificed for the development of the Cathedral." What is the explanation of the attitude of a cathedral where "individuals in animal skins, prancing dancers in leotards" roam the aisles?

Every conceivable pronouncement has been delivered by clergy in our day—from the legalization of marijuana to the legalization of pornography. These pronouncements have been made by bishops even though their own houses have been torn from within by divorce, scandal, and alcoholism. The church has supported every demand made on it, including those by terrorists. Ronald Reagan, in a syndicated column (November 17, 1978), said that the World Council of Churches "is giving us the Gospel According to Karl Marx." He was referring to the Rhodesian terrorists who have received money from Protestant denominations. And many of the people who gave the money did not know where it went.

Unrest in the Christian church is everywhere. There is, indeed, frenzy in the church. What was once respected is now open to criticism. Both bishops and clergy are often in open and heated disagreement. An incident that occurred in a church meeting in Hayward, California, dramatized what can happen. The bishop and the rector engaged in a fight in front of the congregation. Said the rector, "Last night this godly man, who is supposed to be my father in God and is supposed to be our shepherd, phoned me and threatened me and accused me. He was very angry." "I am still angry," retorted the bishop. "He also called me a slimy snake," the rector continued. "An eel," the bishop corrected. Then everyone tried to talk at once. The bishop stalked out of the meeting. Later, the parish voted to secede from the diocese and from the Episcopal church.

Controversies over Charismatics, women priests, prayer books, sexuality, homosexuality, and loss of tradition have resulted in a polarized church.

As we shall see in a later chapter, the charismatic revival now prominent in many of the mainline churches has encouraged free expression in the form of hugging and kissing. Such social encounter is considered a "break" in the normal reverent and quiet mood of a once meditative atmosphere. Thousands are now attending charismatic services where such behavior is considered normal. And many a youth conference is now spiked with a let-your-hair-down "Spirit"-filled party-type experience. At one such youth conference in the Episcopal Diocese of New Jersey an overexuberant youth fell to the ground. Thinking him possessed, the charismatic clergy began to pray for the evil spirit to leave him. The boy was having an epileptic attack. Seeing all this, one sensitive young adult commented, "My God, the church is slap-happy!"

In the name of "relevance" and "bringing the church up-to-date," we are hearing a whole new, casual, and, in many ways, street vocabulary brought into the pulpit and the prayer books. One priest, introducing the use of incense, put it this way, "If you close your eyes, you will smell what Jesus smelled. Now smell it! I'm telling you the truth about this thing. You know I wouldn't screw you."

Some young people who are seeking the ministry are more sensible than their elders who are responsible for their future role in the church. One young man, coming to me for guidance, said that he had been constantly harassed because of his sense of holiness. Trying to cooperate in his local parish, he was subjected to constant verbal abuse by a perpetual deacon. The boy wore a beautiful and tasteful sterling crucifix over his vestment. The deacon snickered, "You go for this stuff because you're easily influenced. Three years from now you'll look at this and laugh. You know why? A crucifix is a dated concept left over from Rome." Holding his temper, the boy replied, "It's almost time for service, may I ring the bell?" The deacon said, "No!" The possibly future seminarian retorted, "Why not?" Abruptly, the deacon declared, "It's not important."

As I have seen many times, clergy like to get their own way. They assume that they know best, and because they are so sure of this a once peaceful parish can be several months under new management and already a nuthouse. Parishioners will be arguing about many things. When the Roman Catholic church declared that all high altars be freestanding (away from the wall) with the priest facing the people to celebrate Mass, many beautiful settings were literally ripped away. Memorials dear to relatives, people who had given thousands of dollars for art work, were then replaced with tables. One priest in Freeburg, Missouri, found his parishioners blocking a moving van that was about to carry off two beautifully carved marble altars. Violence erupted when the moving men started to pull out the ornate sections from the walls of the church. The incident divided the community, which is 98 percent Roman Catholic. The people were aware of the quality of the work in the marble and they also knew that their ancestors "went without shoes to buy those altars."

The attitude of the priest was simply, "The people will have to decide if they want a church or a museum."

The same approach occurred in numerous other orthodox churches, including the Episcopal church, where English style has always been first and foremost. Suddenly, small communities of Christian churchpeople were spending huge amounts in order to redecorate the interiors of their churches. Card tables wound up in front of beautiful sanctuary settings where funds were lacking (while clergy turned their backs on the East). With no knowledge of interior church design or without consultation with architects, clergy have revamped, removed, and rearranged furniture. It was as if to say, "It's all been wrong, but now we will make it right!" One priest even tried to modernize a historic colonial church by attempting to remove the doors from the white pews and changing all the antique colonial lamps—while decking the walls with modern banners and wearing crazy-quilt vestments. It was like going into the Bruton Parish Church in Colonial Williamsburg and slashing about with a free hand.

But sometimes it is the other way around. The people take on the clergy. When they do, God help the pastor. It happened that way in Saint Helen's Parish Church, Rant Broughton, England. BBC technicians were recording a classical guitarist. A bird in the rafters kept chirping. The rector asked all present to leave. Then he had his son shoot the bird.

Women cried, protesting to the Royal Society for the Protection of Birds; national newspapers picked up the story. The entire village turned on the rector. One paper, the *Daily Mirror,* hinted that he might have hit an angel shooting in the air like that. *The Manchester Guardian* printed a letter recommending that they shoot the guitarist and record the bird. Finally, the rector apologized for having committed sparrow murder.

Nothing is so dear to clergy than some personal project. An unusual cause that sprang up in the Episcopal church was the Saint Francis Burial and Counseling Society in Washington, D.C. The concern of this society, of course, is for funeral preparation. From the society one may buy a coffin (available in either kit or assembled form). The brochure published by the society presents traditional or contemporary design for the coffins. Suggestions are offered to make the coffins useful immediately: blanket or quilt storage, a wine-rack accessory package of three shelves (capacity ten bottles), a coffee table, a toy chest, a deacon's bench. If requested, the society can provide plans for "How To Build Your Own Coffin." One church project that went haywire was the effort of the Pauline Fathers to build a shrine in Doylestown, Pennsylvania. An alleged twenty million dollars in donations by the faithful was diverted into business ventures. The *Courier-Post,* April 10, 1980, reported that the criminal fraud investigation was closed without action taken. Headlines complained that the case files were quietly turned over to the bishop of Camden, New Jersey, and his administrative vicar.

Whether clergy witness to their private beliefs about funerals, politics, or social issues, they usually do so with zest. Somehow they know that they have a certain parochial security that doesn't exist for citizens who work in offices or assembly plants. It is not unusual for clergy to leave their flock and carry a placard somewhere for three days. One of the most common witnesses is the fast. To protest evictions from church property during a siege of breakaway churches, the rector of Saint James the Less Church in North Philadelphia lived through a thirty-six-day ordeal without food. At the beginning of his fast, he weighed 217 pounds. When it was over, he weighed sixty pounds. At the end, he was sleeping in the sacristy. Then he wanted to organize, chain-letter fashion, a brotherhood of fasting priests. In an interview he said, "You know, I'm not really the fasting type."

In our day, clergy believe that they have a right to speak out on anything—especially if it is controversial. An Episcopal priest, Rev. Robert Cromey, said, "There ought to be a place where you can come and commit suicide in a dignified way if you want to." In his attempt to sanctify suicide, he continued, "Actually, there have been a considerable number of dignified suicides, such as Saul and Samson in the Bible. These suicides were not criticized because under those circumstances they were making a strong statement as to their own dignity." But this kind of rationale can be made for almost every issue that was once prohibited, including euthanasia, incest, sterilization, sex-change operations, test-tube babies, and cloning.

Bishops have been having trouble not only with themselves but also with their clergy. Rampant divorce and remarriage, misbehavior, and those strange religious quirks that sometimes afflict pietistic pastors who get involved in everything from bleeding statues to blessing tortillas are common occurrences.

It was at Saint Luke's Church in Eddystone, Pennsylvania, that the parish priest went berserk over one of the most "way-out" occurrences in modern church phenomena. It resulted in his suspension and later deposition. He had insisted, in an Episcopal church, on using Latin for the Holy Communion service and on putting a bleeding plaster statue in the church "on instructions from our Lord and our Heavenly Mother." A woman parishioner accused the rector of "stealing the church from the people and doing whatever he wants." After forty-three years as a parishioner, she had turned on her rector. Perhaps she had good reason. The statue originally belonged to a Mrs. Poore. The priest believed that Mrs. Poore was in contact with the "Holy Family." And so people flocked to see the statue at the church. The rector then came to believe himself to be the vicar of Christ on earth, so he began to call himself Bishop Chriszelkial Elias and Pope Peter II. On August 7, 1977, the *Philadelphia Inquirer* magazine, *Today,* printed a feature story on the "New Pope" and a photograph of the miraculous appearance of a communion wafer on Mrs. Poore's tongue. The picture showed her passing the wafer from her tongue to the tongue of the "pope." This tongue-to-tongue communion, in addition to Mrs. Poore's supposed "stigmata," apparently convinced the bishop of Pennsylvania that something had to be done. Facing eviction from the diocese, the "Pope" held his last Easter (1980) service. Standing in the pulpit he shouted, "Let the phonies have the mortar and the bricks." With that dramatic outburst he gave a javelin throw to his bishop's Crozier (Staff) and threw it at the stained glass window behind the altar. This was his act of deconsecration. After service, the congregation retired to the basement for a potluck last supper. His comment about all this was, "There are people out there who will say, they finally got that weirdo . . . but . . . we're going to be resurrected." That was Easter in Eddystone.

Are these religious curiosities simply passing phenomena, or are they indications of some undercurrent of wear in the fabric of what we have known to be sensible religion? They keep surfacing in such numbers and in so many places that it is difficult to see them as isolated incidents. Some sort of trend seems apparent.

In March 1977, following the death of a Canadian priest named Cyrille Labreque, mourners noticed the image of Christ on the sole of his shoe. Soon some fifty thousand people had flocked to see the image on the leather sole when the toe was pointed downward. The shoe is now owned by the Dominican Missionary Adorers Convent at Beauport, Canada. (The priest had helped found the convent.) In death, Father Labreque's left leg remains elevated three inches even after his body was placed in its coffin.

If the imprint of the face of Christ on a shoe sole seems bizarre, then read on, for Jesus seems to be appearing in even more unlikely places these days.

Lois Linden saw Christ in her kitchen window screen. Her house in Delcambre, Lousiana. was so besieged by people that police had to tow away cars. It triggered a surge of visions in the town, including people who claimed the weathervane on Our Lady of the Lake Catholic Church gave off a glow and pointed in the direction of Mrs. Linden's house. His features have appeared on altar cloths, shadows on houses and walls, within the branches of trees, and, believe it or not, on a tortilla. (I am open to the thought of all possible kinds of paranormal manifestations. But a tortilla!) Maria Rubio, in Lake Arthur, New Mexico, was preparing the flour for her husband's tortilla when, she says, "I noticed something which looked like a face." She took the tortilla to church the day after the appearance. After she had kept it for six days, the image was still intact. So—if you want to see Jesus on a tortilla, which is surely more impressive than Jesus in plastic on the dashboard of a car, you will have to visit Mrs. Rubio. (According to an article in the August 2, 1978, *Philadelphia Inquirer,* more than eight thousand people have done so.) Perhaps the shrine that Mrs. Rubio is going to build will be called the Shrine of the Divine Tortilla.

Mrs. Rubio's priest considered the whole drama a coincidence, but he proceeded to bless the tortilla anyhow. Mrs. Rubio herself considers the event a "miracle." And the tortilla is now surrounded by holy pictures and burning candles.

The tortilla event poses many questions: will someone see Jesus on a McDonald's Big Mac? Will someone see His face in an ice cube floating in a vodka tonic? (How could they convince anyone when the cube melted?) Will He appear on a pancake or a pizza? Will there be bumper stickers that proclaim "I've seen Him!" instead of "I've found it!" Will a misbehaving Fundamentalist see Jesus' face in the midst of a spinning roulette wheel at Atlantic City?

A certain thirty-seven-year-old nun from New York certainly didn't see it. Instead it is reported that she had her purse stolen while playing the nickel slot machine at the Stardust Hotel in Las Vegas.

The strange thing about all these incidents is that the face of Jesus always looks like the face on the Shroud of Turin. And that's really something to think about.

The accounts and the experiences of clergy not being able to control their own lives leave many churches shattered in faith and morale. People still expect their priest or minister to be someone whom they can hold in high esteem. What they themselves cannot be, or even hope to be, they want to see in their pastor. Any person who enters the ministry must expect that he cannot be in the pulpit and the pew at the same time. His unconscious self may want the world, but he cannot have it. He may insist that all his people call him Father Joe or Pastor Jack or Reverend Rick. He may wear a clerical collar with an orange shirt and a yellow suit. But he is still what he set out to be: a minister, not a layman. No matter that clergy attire nowadays can vary from the formal black suit to a collar, plaid jacket, a plaid clerical front—and shorts. He is still a minister. One clergyman visiting a bereaved friend of mine was dressed totally in green except for his white clerical collar. Wearing green shirt, suit, socks, and pocket handkerchief, he approached her at the funeral home and said, "Hello there, I'm Father Green."

To be sure, the occupational hazards of the ministry today can be very great. Sometimes there is danger in the pulpit, in counseling, or in just wearing the collar. A good example of this is the case of Rev. Bernard T. Pagano, of Wilmington, Delaware. He was identified as the "gentlemen bandit" who worked with a silver handgun, finally winding up in the police lineup. Parishioners and friends took sides for his guilt or innocence. And Father Pagano was the subject of national publicity until the real bandit at last confessed and the charges were dropped. The nightmare finally ended for Father Pagano, even though the newspapers delighted in recalling that his former parish was Saint Mary, Refuge of Sinners.

Clergy also run the risk, nowadays, of being sued for "malpractice." One pastor advised a woman to leave her husband. He immediately sued the pastor for aiding in the breakup of his marriage.

Some companies are now adding "counselors' liability"

to the lists of insurance they sell. In Merrill, Wisconsin, the Church Mutal Insurance Company is doing just that. So is Preferred Risk Insurance of Des Moines, Iowa.

People sue churches. Leaving a wedding at my church, a woman missed the step, fell, and split her head against a vestibule radiator. She refused to go to the emergency room at the local hospital. But later she sued.

At the First Baptist Church in Biloxi, Mississippi, during Easter services in 1974, a layman took the pulpit. He then shot his dog and himself in full view of the congregation.

A New York City rector told me of several instances when a stranger appeared in front of the altar, stared, and left. No explanation, no conversation. Just a long, silent stare.

I myself have had a knife pulled on me, have been shoved, threatened, and spat upon in vain attempts to help strangers at the church door.

In Littleton, New Hampshire, a Roman Catholic priest, Rev. Joseph Sands, was shot to death by a couple who claimed to be the "King and Queen of the Church."

In San Salvador, Archbishop Oscar Romero was celebrating Mass when he was murdered at the altar in a hospital chapel reminiscent of Saint Thomas à Becket of Canterbury.

In Daingerfield, Texas a geometry teacher "kicked in the doors" of the First Baptist Church during worship services and yelled, "This is war!" He opened fire with a "semi-automatic weapon." People dove under the pews, screamed and scattered. Five parishioners were killed and eleven were injured, seven of which were admitted to the hospital.

A good friend of mine, the Reverend Dr. Schone Setzer, in a counseling session on a Thanksgiving day, was murdered in front of his family by a man who plunged a knife into his heart while he was praying.

These incidents do not include those that have to do with the personal problems of clergymen. Such personal problems or pressures result in things like the murder at the parsonage in Milwaukee because of a lover's triangle that involved the minister.

The wife of a rector in Columbia, South Carolina, used a baseball bat and a butcher knife to kill her priest-husband. Other incidents are of tragic suicides, such as that of the assistant rector of Saint Chrysostom's Church in Chicago, who plunged to his death from the twenty-seventh floor of the Continental Plaza Hotel. Or the assistant at the Long Island Episcopal Cathedral who hung himself. Other tragedies include the priest brother of one of my own parishioners, who was murdered during a robbery at the rectory; or a seminary friend who was beaten to death with a lead pipe.

The Episcopal church seems to have courted more tortuous situations for itself than most denominations. It has suffered through enormous turmoil and even bailed itself out of the most involved situations of misconduct. One such situation involved $35,000 from the presiding bishop's discretionary fund, which was presented to two women, who were jailed for ten months, in 1977. They worked for the national headquarters of the church and were involved in a probe of terrorist activities of a Puerto Rican nationalist group. The two women served as executive director and secretary of the church's Commission on Hispanic Affairs. In connection with requested information on terrorist bombings they would not testify before a grand jury. They then charged the church with "betraying" their cause.

Battle after battle has raged in modern times as Christians have trod the King's Highway. One that rages on with an after-the-fact cloudy sky all around it is the issue of women priests. We shall be looking at this one in more detail in a later chapter, but it should be reviewed here.

Unthinkable, but nevertheless a fact, the now infamous Philadelphia Episcopal ordination of eleven women in 1974 has created ripples that still spread through the sanctuaries of churches across the land. Because of it, lawsuits, demands, accusations, and vigorous statements pro and con still divide clergy and laity. The ordination of those eleven priestesses created much of the frenzy in the church that we know today.

The frenzy is just beginning in the Roman Catholic church. It became most public when a nun stood up to tell the pope the "truth" during his appearance at Washington's Shrine of the Immaculate Conception.

Rev. Elizabeth Weisner, an Episcopalian, was interviewed in London after having preached at Westminster Abbey. She said, "I can understand how a man gets crabby if he gets up early for communion and finds himself faced with a woman priest. He knows that Christ came in male form. He speaks of God the Father. But I believe Christ had male and female qualities. He came in male form because it was right at that time, but his penis wasn't an essential part of his attributes."

An interesting statement was made by Rev. Jacqueline Means (who calls herself Mother Means) when she was asked if she would like to become the first woman bishop. She replied, "It would be kinda neat!"

Much of the feminist gospel preached by women priests has to do with rights. Canon Mary Michael Simpson's call for sexual equality in the Christian church reached seven hundred worshippers in Westminster Abbey. Even so, the Church of England, along with the Roman Catholic pope, rejects women priests.

But this has not stopped the march for church rights for women in America, where no bishop is safe from a lawsuit brought by some ordination-minded female. Other battles related to this one are seen in the ongoing debates about human sexuality, abortion, and birth control.

In another direction, the frenzy in the church is seen in the fact that this is an age that fears piety but wants to wear T-shirts emblazoned with such phrases as "Heaven or Hell?"

"Turn or Burn," and wants to put bumper stickers on its cars, admonishing, "If you love Jesus, honk!"

It is an age when Jewish mothers don't want their children coming home from school singing "Silent Night." And Christian mothers don't want their kids celebrating Chanukah. So—we have no religious celebrations in public schools, tradition to the contrary.

It is an age of confusion of basic English. Rev. Kenneth D. Aldrich, of Red Bank, New Jersey, calls it "seduction by semantics," and he has devised the following list of examples of what he means:

What used to be called modesty is now called a sex hangup.

What used to be called Christian discipline is now called unhealthy repression.

What used to be called disgusting is now called adult.

What used to be called moral irresponsibility is now called being freed up.

What used to be called chastity is now called neurotic inhibitions.

What used to be called self-indulgence is now called self-fulfillment.

What used to be called living in sin is now called a meaningful relationship.

What used to be called perversion is now called alternate life-style.

What used to be called depravity is now called creative self-expression.

What used to be called ethical anarchy is now called the theology of liberation.

Where do the established churches really stand on all these issues? What is the sense and nonsense in religion today? What is the future of the church and of religion as we know it? Where is the hope that we have all been taught to uphold and reach out to grasp?

These are some of the areas and some of the questions to be covered in the following pages. While you read this book, it will be useful to remember some statistics about America and American religions:

In 1978, the Gallup Poll reported that "some 61 million American adults are not members of any church or religious institution." But in an address in 1976 before the Episcopal Radio-TV Foundation in Atlanta, George Gallup reported the results of a worldwide survey in which Americans emerged as the most religious people in the contemporary world; that is, they were "among the advanced nations in terms of importance placed on religion and in terms of the levels of belief in God and an afterlife."

Even though our crime rate is high compared to those of other nations, Gallup believes that religion "may indeed be the glue that holds our democracy together." But even though it may hold our democracy together, the religion of the churches is having a declining influence, indicating that if there is indeed a religious revival, it is not necessarily from the church itself but from an undercurrent—one in fact so hard to understand that it must be from the Holy Spirit somewhere deep in the lives of men and women.

CHAPTER TWO

TO HELL WITH AUTHORITY

Orderliness is essential to all facets of life if any society is to maintain discipline and have protection. It is therefore incredible to observe the disorder and lack of discipline that characterizes the church today.

Authority suffers when no one pays attention to it. The loose structure that has developed in the Episcopal church and that is beginning to be apparent in the United Presbyterian church, among others of the mainline denominations, is the end result of liberty banishing rule. People are no longer paying attention to authority and certainly not to the authority of the church. They admire Pope John Paul II, wait in long lines to see him, and then reject his authority.

Rev. Robert J. Center wrote, in an article in *The Living Church* magazine: "The Episcopal Church is in jeopardy . . . from wilful violation of its order . . . by those bound to uphold it." He believes that the violation began publicly with the ordination of the Philadelphia Eleven. People sense that there is no need to obey canon law when their bishops do not obey it. It is as simple as that.

A further breakdown of authority in the church is demonstrated by the attacks on it by those who have further disobeyed secular authority and, having no spiritual sense, violate the church. Churches were once open at all hours in town and city. No more. The famous Washington Cathedral now has twenty-four security guards. It spends $200,000 a year guarding the house of the Lord. At one time a person could pray at the cathedral any time. Now the great doors close at six p.m.

Broken windows, stolen tapestries, looted money boxes, obscene graffiti on carved stone—all these are mute evidence of the breakdown of authority today. *U.S. News and World Report,* in its April 21, 1975 issue, detailed violence in our churches in a two-page spread. The article listed everything from stolen sound systems to the robbery of a congregation of four hundred worshippers who were forced to lie on the floor as they were systematically stripped of anything of value.

In a church known to me, the rector's own son stole the sound equipment. Another rector's son was arrested for burglary and the attempted rape of a parishioner. When I was a member of the Trinity Cathedral Chapter, in Trenton, New Jersey, it was not at all uncommon to consider over and over again the problem of the once-again broken stained glass windows. Finally a huge sum was expended for Lexan to cover the priceless glass. My own church has been vandalized, set afire, robbed of valuable items, and had its baptismal font filled with urine.

But physical acts of vandalism and violence may be only the outward signs of a deep cancer within our society and the body of the church itself.

The Right Reverend John E. Hines, former presiding bishop, said recently that "the Episcopal Church is 'tired' and 'uncomfortable in a collapsing world.' . . . the Church was alive from 1967 to 1973, but it has pretty well died since then." He went on to say that the cause of its demise was "that we created in Seattle in 1967 as a symbol of the necessity of the Church's engagement with the world, the General Convention Special Program through which millions were spent on projects to aid minorities.

"We tried," Bishop Hines said, "to take money and expertise and help empower groups to gain both political and economic prominence and power in our society. We didn't care if they became Episcopalians or not. In a sense, we didn't care whether they became Christians. We did care that they had the freedom and option to choose . . . that made some people mad as hell. Some cut off their contributions to the Church. We dealt with many a minority group that was edging toward violence in a society which had rejected them. And now the Church is tired and wants to retreat into the womb of comfortableness and wait out the siege."

Bishop Hines described himself as "a hard-nosed guy" in regard to those who have left the church and set up new churches over such issues as women's ordination, social involvement, and revision of the Book of Common Prayer. "I don't belong to the reconciling element in the Episcopal Church," he said. "If they want to come back, fine. We've still got enough s.o.b.'s in the Church to be able to accommodate some more. But if they do come back or not doesn't worry me."

The whole problem of authority is seen quite clearly in the unrest among Roman Catholic priests and scholars. A newspaper headline reads: "Pope Orders Jesuits To Toe The Line." And in the article that follows, it is reported that "many young Jesuits in the United States don't believe in life after death, don't believe Jesus to be the Son of God, and even skip Mass on Sundays." Some Jesuits, even high-ranking ones, "have accepted a Marxist analysis of society in a profound way."

As I write this book, the headlines in Europe and America are full of the "heresy" trials of Roman Catholic theologians Edward Schillebeeckx, of Holland, and Hans Küng, of Germany. Both have been summoned to Rome to be questioned by the Congregation for the Doctrine of Faith, which is the latter-day successor of the Inquisition. In essence, the case against both men is that they do not submit to the doctrinal authority of Pope John Paul II. And even before his "trial," Professor Küng has been stripped of his authority as a Catholic theologian for "continued contempt of church doctrine." In his books, Küng has questioned papal infallibility, the authority of bishops, mandatory priestly celibacy, and church opposition to birth control.

A year or so ago, Paul Seabury, a descendant of Bishop Samuel Seabury, of Connecticut, the first Episcopal bishop in the United States, wrote an article entitled "Trendier Than Thou." [1] His comments annoyed a great many clergy who considered themselves "with it." In the article, Seabury simply detailed the developing trends in what he said was once a sensible church. When it was published, one bishop waved it at his clergy and told them to read it because it was "filled with errors." Perhaps there were errors, but the trends themselves were dramatically spelled out. Moreover, those trends continue to evolve in a once conservative church. The cover of the issue of *Harper's* magazine, in which the article appeared, featured the bright red lips of a woman and part of her face, and a neck wearing a clerical collar. It was a symbol of "liberation." To hell with authority in the Episcopal church.

As the Episcopal church began to fragment, individual congregations began to split. Led by rectors, they were marched down the paths of loyalty or disloyalty, depending on their ideas of church tradition. Some ultra-Catholic and archconservative priests and laity decided that they couldn't take it. The higher leadership of their church no longer represented what they stood for. And so authority broke down between clergy and bishops. Local churches abandoned the authority of the diocese. Diocesan authority lost all control of churches. Striking out on their own, local congregations fought with their dioceses over their buildings and eventually wound up in court. The legal battles became test cases. In the end, most diocesan authorities won their buildings but lost their priests and congregations.

So intent were these priests that some of them started their own branch of the Episcopal church, seeking financial backing from dedicated laymen and wealthy sponsors. They started new dioceses and gave new names to churches, most of which now meet in homes of the members. In a kind of clandestine ecclesiastical trick, these conservatives are consecrating bishops, ordaining priests, and creating seminaries. Such new "parishes" as Saint Anselm of Canterbury or Saint Charles the Martyr go on as fragmented Catholic-oriented groups.

Several of my own seminary classmates have left the church entirely because they feel that it is not the same church into which they were ordained. Many other priests feel the same way but have not left, believing that even though there is disunity one cannot be part of something that does not have a true historical continuity. One priest who left and started his own church was simply removed from the pension fund by the diocese as soon as possible. In the diocesan headquarters, the comment was, "Well, that will take care of him!"

Many schismatic clergy wanted authority, but not in the form it has presently taken. What they saw was a badly mixed-up authority. They saw bishops as authority figures but without real authority, not even respect for the token authority they did have.

The Reverend Dr. Earl Brill, director of studies at the College of Preachers, Washington, D.C., treats the exodus of clergy and churches as deserving only minimal attention. He believes that it will not amount to much because, like replacing a cell, these people will be replaced by others. Time will tell. The truth is that right now the shores of the Episcopal church are strewn with the wrecks of disillusioned priests.

I have used the above examples because I am most familiar with the inner workings of my own church. But the same story can easily be recounted by anyone who knows the condition of the United Presbyterians, the United Methodists, the American Baptists, and the Lutheran church in America.

Schismatic trends are discernible in all of the branches of the Christian Church around the world. It is not necessary to talk with those who have already left the church. Any serious conversation with those who have remained in their local churches will reveal that these people, ordained and laity, are slowly thinking about the new forces at work in their hearts and minds which they are told are "the new winds of the Holy Spirit." They are the whisperings of a supreme sweep of renewal, it is said. But I have heard clergymen of a number of different denominations say, "I'm not leaving the church, the church is leaving me!" In fact, those were the exact words spoken by Rev. James Mote of Saint Mary's Episcopal Church in Denver. He and his congregation seceded, the first to do so, in 1976. They would not recognize the authority of the bishop because they felt that the whole church had abandoned doctrine, discipline, and worship. The bishop then exercised his authority. He suspended Mote from all priestly functions. In another instance, the Rev. James Sharp was forbidden, by written decree, all priestly functions in his Grand Rapids, Michigan, parish. He refused to use the new prayer book. Father Sharp publicly burned the bishops' authoritative letter while his parishioners applauded. A cathedral canon was sent to rescue the parish. They would not let him in.

Even within the newly formed Anglican church in America, the conflict with authority has already reared its head. This is the church that was formed by those not satisfied that their new church was Catholic enough. So the Laymen's League was formed as "an organization of Lay Catholics (Episcopal) dedicated to the restoration of full corporate unity of an Anglican jurisdiction subject to the See of Rome; and resolved, with God's help, so to proclaim the Catholic religion, so to pray daily for unity and for the Holy Father . . . we so dedicate and resolve ourselves, subject to the direction of the Diocese of Saint Augustine of Canterbury and the will of the Holy See." The Anglo-Catholic movement thus surfaced again almost as another church. And certainly created another problem for the tired and bedraggled Episcopal church.

Corporate authority in the House of Bishops is now in question by numerous clergy who look to the mind of the church and the custodians of the Holy Mysteries as being unable to agree on issues that shape the future.

The bishops from time to time issue a pastoral letter to the congregations of the church. It is a letter upon which all bishops should agree. But it is clear that in many cases they do not agree. Even so, the letter is written in such a way as to appear acceptable. Some statements are quite definite, but on many occasions the great issues of our time are left open.

The Urban Bishops' Coalition of The Episcopal Church (a separate group of bishops concerned with urban problems) issued a Labor Day message in 1979. They "commended the letter to be read in place of a sermon." The letter was replete with words such as economic contraction, rejuvenation, gentrification, and deprivation. It called for just about everything from plant closings to a moratorium on the development of nuclear weapons and the "eradication of racism, sexism and poverty." It looked like a pastoral letter from all the bishops of the church, but it wasn't.

Anyone can send out anything in the Episcopal church these days, and the unsuspecting laity will accept it as the whole church speaking. It is easy to obtain a printout of addresses. One magazine of the avant-garde calls itself *The*

Witness, but lists itself as The Episcopal Church Publishing Company. The editors of the magazine speak with authority on issues such as "Revolution with Marx and Jesus," "The Politics of Advent," and "Confessions of a Midwest Macho Liberal." They espouse the denial of authority in what Americans know as democracy.

In the Spring 1976 issue of *The Witness* an article called "The Shackles of Domination and Oppression" by Michael Manley, prime minister of Jamaica, tells how democracy has failed in a capitalist system. The message is clear that our system is one of oppression. He wrote: "I do not believe that Western Christendom can cease from struggle until these outrages that violate our religious faith and mock its teaching have been totally overthrown and abolished. Every politician and every churchman, indeed, everyone who neither raises his hand nor his voice against such systems of oppression thereby betrays the very cause of justice." [2]

It seems to me that the effort to break down authority and to use the church to accomplish that breakdown can reverse-feed the breakdown of the authority of government, the home, and the school. When this happens, the authority of the church is the first to succumb.

When the founding fathers established this nation they did so under the divine protection and guidance of the Grand Architect of the Universe, a Supreme Being, a God, who was at work with square and compasses in the formation of this country. We were free. But we were not free from that authority which would help govern and guide, in an honest way, in behalf of what was always recognized as a higher authority. The people were free, but not free to use freedom as a cloak for maliciousness. They recognized authority and even in their various church backgrounds saw it as essential. They also saw the emerging democracy as incomplete, something yet to be fulfilled in the Divine Plan. For that very reason, they left the capstone off the pyramid of the dollar bill as a symbol. The future would fill in the empty spaces. They designed a flag where stars symbolizing the states occupied a blue field, a message that God was in the picture. On their coins, they inscribed, "In God We Trust." Thus any breakdown in authority in our day, either in respect to government or to religion, is an evidence of gray skies that were once bright with promise.

Clergy are, therefore, authority figures. The fact that priests are called "Father" infers a parental concern. Jesus himself presented God as Father, as one who cares for all his children. And the implication is that when Father speaks, children should obey. That is the ideal. It is assumed that the Father has wisdom and speaks the truth; he can be trusted. It is thus inferred that when clergy speak, they have a built-in audience. Not that their voice is as strong as it was years ago, but that there is still an inherent respect among the laity for the clergy. If a clergyman who has authority speaks against the authority of others, his listeners are forced to choose.

Such was the case when Canon Walter B. Dennis—now a bishop—advocated the legalization of marijuana. Although he did not believe that the drug should be advertised, he thought that there could be "some form of regulated distribution . . . and the tax revenue from sales used to further some positive benefit to the public." He said, "I believe that we have passed the point where the 'harmfulness' of marijuana is the central or even the viable issue."

The fact is that this same kind of justification for the use of marijuana (and many other drugs) is now being heard from the pulpits of churches of all the major denominations. But since medical as well as theological opinion does not speak with one voice on the matter, laymen are forced to choose. It seems to me, on the basis of my experience with young people and on my theological understanding, that the use of drugs cannot be justified. In the Genesis story we are to understand that man is put into a holistic situation in which he has all that he needs for health, but he has ruined it for himself. The authority of a loving God underlies the story—as long as Adam and Eve cooperated with nature, all would be well. But it is just this authority that is put into question when people must choose between dissenting clergymen.

We all have a need for authority as well as a built-in tendency to reject it. And rejection of the authority of religion is easy when the ordained representatives of religion do not know how to represent it properly. In the English diocese of Norwich, there are "mobile priests" riding motorcycles and wearing crash helmets. When the program was initiated, the bishop blessed all the motorbikes and they roared off to their duties. Did they realize that they had adopted a police look and attitude? And is it police authority that the church is called upon to emulate? (Someone called the whole affair "a rodeo of reverend gentlemen.") If authority is either misused or misrepresented, the church puts itself in a position that is as untenable as it is ridiculous.

Professor James E. Griffiss, of Nashotah House (an Episcopal seminary), recently delivered an address on "The Anglican Experience of Authority." In it he stated that much of what is happening today is "not simply the questioning of a particular understanding of the ordained ministry; it is a questioning of the foundation of that ministry itself." The reasons for the problem of the conflict of authority in the church, said Professor Griffiss, are multifaceted: "The development of scientific humanism, the critical examination of the origin of Christianity, atheistic philosophy, and, most important of all, a dominant cultural materialism."

As I have indicated earlier, I believe that the crisis is not only in the church, but also in the government. It is both secular and religious. But, as Professor Griffiss pointed out in his address, "We who are Christians claim or acknowledge an authority beyond all forms of secular authority." That is, our danger is not only in losing sight of secular authority but more especially of rejecting the authority of Christ who is our Lord, our Standard, our Sign. Knowing Christ gives us freedom, but it does not allow us to ignore authority either from heaven or earth. Both worlds operate at the same time in our lives. For that very reason, in seeking the ways of heaven, Christians must maintain order in the ways of earth.

And so, in the end, we *cannot* simply say, "To hell with authority." Because, of course, it is not a question of whether or not we shall have authority. The question is: Whose authority shall we live under, man's or God's?

As Christians, we already know the answer to that question. But most of us must come to it the long way round. To understand the full implications of this, let me refer again to the speech made by Professor Griffiss. He says: "The problem is this: How do we, historical, finite, temporal, limited and sinful human beings understand and appropriate in our lives the Mystery of the eternal, unknowable, and absolutely transcendent God who has become Man?" Once we understand the nature of that question, the answer to our problem with authority, whether between the various ranks of the clergy or between clergy and laity, should come clear.

The question is, finally, only this: How do we know God's will for us?

Professor Griffiss has some useful words on that point:

> Only as the question of God's will is faced squarely and honestly can we then accept squarely and honestly that the Mystery of God is something that we shall never grasp fully and which we shall never express adequately. That mystery is shown to us through the many different, often conflicting ways in which the Church and Christian people have witnessed to it in every generation and in every time and place both in their doctrinal formulation and in their lives. I believe that we do know this truth in our personal lives as we try to live out the life in Christ. We know, for example, in the ambiguity in which we must live and act most of the time, that our decisions are fre-

quently wrong, our motives are always mixed, that what we hope for is confused, that our love for one another is never pure, and even that our faith is rarely perfect.

But yet we also know from our personal experience that it is precisely in that pilgrimage of faith, in which we rarely know where we are coming from and where we are going, that God's will becomes clear to us. *In the midst of all our uncertainty, all our ambiguity, we know that there is only one thing certain, to which we must hold lest we die, and that is, that in Christ God has redeemed us and that he will accomplish his purpose in us.* (Italics mine.) [3]

No. We cannot say, "To hell with authority." However much dissension we see in the church today, however much flouting of authority there may be, in the end it is God's authority, because God's will *can* be known for us and by us.

CHAPTER THREE

MALE OR FEMALE

W hat could be more unusual in these times than a pastor or priest having a sex-change operation? But it has happened in the United States and in England; it may well have happened elsewhere.

An English vicar, name withheld by officials, became a woman. Living in the diocese of Blackburn, northern England, he was unmarried and middle-aged. After the operation he resigned and gave up the priesthood. The fact that women cannot be priests in the Church of England posed too many complicated problems for him/her. In fact, whether or not becoming a woman after a transsexual operation affects the ordination of a person is still a question!

The Right Reverend Robert A. S. Martineau apparently answered the questions of many when he referred to the priest or priestess in respect to prayer. "Almighty God will know for whom the prayer is made."

The same kind of event took place in Colorado when a Catholic priest, William Griglak, at age forty-seven, became Nancy Ledens. After a life that included depression and despair, marriage and divorce, and which culminated in the separation of his priestly functions, Father Griglak finally decided that "the operation was an attempt to become what we always thought we were." He told church officials, "I feel I should be a girl."

Sex has always been a mystery to conjure with. It is a never-ending array of tidbits that the press plays games with, an endless source of supply for gossipers in every community, the prattle of TV talk shows, and the internal conversation of clergy and official church headquarters.

Although Europe has a relaxed attitude toward most areas of sexual behavior, the United States, with its built-in "puritanical" background and its porno parlors and TV talk shows that daily showcase sex is still reticent about facing the facts of life—especially at the level of small towns and villages. Consequently, the rise in sex literature, as well as in public conversation, has made more people aware of the sorcery of sex at every level than ever before. People who never thought about what other people did in the bedroom are now judging each other. And the sex battle is one of the great battles now raging in the churches.

Clergy often assume that their people are obsessed with sex. Thus they inflict on their parishioners countless seminars, group discussions, and sermons on the subject. And they also try to project their own views of the intimate behavior of the bedroom.

Major denominations have appointed commissions to study and report on the subject of human sexuality. Sex-rights groups parade and demand equality regardless of the teaching of Holy Scripture.

Some clergy have openly declared what they have held hidden for years. In a Congregational church in Orange, Massachusetts, the minister felt that he should include in his sermon the information that he was a homosexual. And he announced the sermon in advance. Even though his wife accepted the situation, this did not soothe the anxieties of the married members of his flock. Finally, the minister and his wife packed up their children and moved to an area where he could minister to "gay Christians" in the Gay Metropolitan Community Church.

So unsettling has the subject of homosexuality become that the Minnesota Supreme Court has upheld a ruling of a lower court that Big Brothers, Inc. can now ask potential big brothers about their "sexual preference." The officers of the group felt the need to "protect" the children they are trying to help.

The blessing of "gay unions" has become a battle issue, for instance, in Hamilton Village, Philadelphia, where priests have the endorsement of their vestry to conduct such blessings.

Yes, sex in church is a popular subject today. Marriage, divorce, and even a "non-sexist" version of the Bible all have overtones of a flesh-conscious church struggling with its own image. In Methodist churches, the betrothed couple may choose whether the wedding service will imply a later divorce. A recently authorized ritual for divorce "calls for the estranged couple to stand before the minister with the congregation present." The wedding band is then transferred from the left hand to the right. They are then no longer married in the Lord. They are divorced in the Lord.

So many authors have submitted sexually obscene manuscripts dealing with religious subjects that many publishers no longer read them beyond the first few pages. In the midst of this the once-revered Seabury Press, longtime official publishing house of the Episcopal church, got in the sex act by printing a controversial 500-page *Sex Atlas*. One priest said he thought the presiding bishop should see the book, but it could not be sent through the mail! Proposed films, such as *The Many Faces of Jesus,* if ever produced, will show the Lord having both homosexual and heterosexual relationships. Sex-conscious clergy are trying in vain to rid the language of the church of all reference to male or female. One priest begins the Lord's Prayer by saying, "Our Creator in heaven . . ." One president of the Episcopal Churchwomen said, "If we look at God as feminine, what would males be? But if we see God as masculine, are women thereby inferior? Christians cannot possibly support either position." The debate rages on.

Perhaps the most pressing debate is the one over homosexuality. A *Time* essay, January 8, 1979, summed up what many people are trying to balance out in their own minds: tolerance versus approval. The essay details a strong reaction to the homosexual rights movement, attitudes to other cultures, psychological studies, attitudes of parents, inhuman treatment of gays, and the ever-present feelings of fear that still dominate many who are involved in the sexual revolution.

Several of the denominations have produced studies on sexuality such as that of the United Presbyterian General Assembly. The subject is of continuing concern at the annual meetings of these churches. During the closing session of the assembly in 1978, the delegates defeated a proposal to grant some official standing to a group known as the "Presbyterian Gay Concern." Likewise, no official standing was or will be given to such associations as "Integrity, Inc." of the Episcopal church and "Dignity" of the Roman Catholic church. All of these groups—which seek favor and thrust what they believe to be burning issues into the church policy machine—eventually become like the proverbial horse with blinders. They see only what is directly before them.

In Great Britain, the annual 1979 meeting in London of the Methodist church was faced with a study that certainly characterized "the spirit of the age." The report based on the study ruled out "trial marriages" but acknowledged "stable permanent relationships."

A repairman working in my church told me that a new minister had just been installed in his own church. The first thing the new pastor did was start a five-week group discussion on sexuality. The repairman said to me, "What the hell do I need that for—all this sex stuff? What is he—frustrated or something?"

In a permissive society there is need for discussion. But to what extent and how? The addiction to love can be understood in many ways, and the Christian should understand that diversity. Perhaps C. S. Lewis best described the various ways in which human love manifests itself. In his book, *The Four Loves,* he discusses *storge, eros, philia,* and *agape,* the four Greek words that are used in the Bible to indicate the various meanings which English tries to cram into the words "sex" and "love." Professor Lewis's book is recommended reading!

A Methodist pastor, Rev. Alson J. Smith, reviews the various expressions of love in his monograph "The Basic Principles of Spiritual Discipline," pointing out that spiritual discipline is impossible without love. And he also makes the point that such love must be without worldliness, without erotic love. It must be what the New Testament calls *agape:* the love that held together the people of the early church. It is the love that seeks union with God, the love that Jesus felt for the Father, the essence of what we know as the love of God.

Today, the church seems preoccupied with the place of *eros* in its life, rather than with *agape.* Yet it is clear that *agape*-love is a prerequisite for any deep spiritual understanding and continuing spiritual exercise. *Agape* is God and God is *Agape.* When immature, unpredictable *eros* has been transmuted into the higher, nobler *agape,* we are then ready to practice the presence of God.

Even though the church has wrestled with the distinction between physical sex and so-called Christian sex, it still faces the charge that it is behind the times. People inside and outside the church are saying that the church must allow for more "free expression" in all forms of sexuality and in all manner of living. Nevertheless, as Rev. James G. Hodder has observed, "Christianity not only says that sex experience must be sacred, romantic, deeply personal, it must also, to fufill its function of glorifying God in our bodies, be socially responsible. Sex is our link to the past and our link to the future. No Christian should enter into it without a deep and lasting sense of the sheer wonder of ongoing life. In the mystery of sex is hidden the mystery of new life, and only the shallow soul can be careless before that mystery." [1]

The real issue in all of today's battles over sex is the problem of what C. D. Keys has called "sex and transcendence." This involves the so-called rights (which are already there) that the homosexual community is fighting for in the realm of religion. Unfortunately, in the mind of the public as well as in the minds of many homosexuals, there is more sex than transcendence. Perhaps I see it most often and more clearly in my own parish because Anglicanism is the most antipuritanical branch of Christendom.

Following Anita Bryant's controversial crusade, the printing presses of religion-land turned out material on every conceivable aspect of the subject of homosexuality. Church magazines began to review two and three books on the subject in each issue; study commissions cranked out reports by the dozen. All of the church newspapers of every denomination in the land printed articles by every expert they could find.

The subject also engendered a subtle witch-hunt, an undercurrent of suspicion, and a strong surge of prejudice. The possibility of character assassination lurked in the background of conversations of people about other people. This has sometimes turned on the notion that new pastors should be married, the implication being that if they are not married they must be gay.

One diocesan commission on ministry, when interviewing candidates, is intent on asking questions about sex. Such questions seem to be more important to the members of the commission than are the reasons why a person feels that he has a vocation. In fact, a member of the commission told me, "The first thing we look for is the sex thing." But what they are looking for is not even what many aspirants to the ministry are thinking of at all. The point is that Christians all agree that the church should have a pastoral concern for the homosexual, but laymen, when placed on committees to study the problem or deal with it in a person-to-person situation, are very often in over their heads—without credentials.

The General Convention of the Episcopal church asked every diocese to appoint a commission to study the issue of human sexuality. In six months the church was totally immersed in a flood of material on sex. Church members were asked to study the subject from the biological, psychological, legal, ethical, and theological dimensions. Material was gathered from any and every source. Some dioceses came up with so many resolutions that it would have taken an entire convention on sex just to deal with the findings.

The United Presbyterian Church alone produced a "Blue Book" on the subject; it ran to more than 200 pages. It was a comprehensive study by the "Task Force on Homosexuality" and was presented to the 190th General Assembly in 1978. But the eminent Professor Bruce Metzger of Princeton Theological Seminary found the report "seriously deficient in a number of important areas." The many disputes among psychologists, psychiatrists, and even local congregations prompted the recommendation that the report be rejected on the point of ordination of homosexuals.

At its 1979 general convention in Denver, the Episcopal church passed a resolution that practicing homosexual persons should not be ordained. Ninety-nine bishops voted for the resolution, and thirty-four voted against it. Even the bishops of the Episcopal church cannot agree on the mystery of sex!

The "no" bishops then proceeded to issue a kind of split-house pastoral statement of their own. Prior to all the studies, the bishop of New York had openly ordained an avowed lesbian, thus igniting the flames of controversy in congregations across the land. Almost immediately, a glut of books on lesbian life appeared. Many of these books approached the subject seriously and sympathetically. Their authors hoped to defeat the stereotype view that lesbians are tragic and disturbed women who are always trying to convert others to their life-style. They showed clearly that if there are any oppressive effects of these various life-styles, those effects come from society and not from the lesbian herself.

Sometimes the condition of homosexuality so alienates the "Christian" community that a person can be denied a theological degree. This happened at Lexington Theological Seminary in Kentucky. In 1976, Circuit Court Judge Charles Tackett ruled that one young man, even though a homosexual, was entitled to his degree, despite the wishes of the seminary administration, because he had indeed completed the academic requirements. The judge said: "If the seminary intends to deny degrees to homosexuals, adulterers, agnostics, thieves or others, it should say so in its catalogue with sufficient clarity."

The history of the subject of homosexuality has been dealt with mostly in underground books, and such studies were not usually available in local paperback bookshops. But times have changed. Our present era has produced books that try to give a comprehensive survey of sexuality, including its religious implications. We are more "informed" about sex today than any civilization has ever been. A well-read parishioner recently said to me, "I'm sick and tired of reading about sex and the church." In one issue alone, *Christian Century* magazine reviewed ten books on "The Church and Gays." Conservatives, liberals, and liberationists all had their say. And, of course, the subject has also been grist for the mills of both humorists and artists. A Canadian paper showed a cartoon vicar holding a handbag while greeting his flock. One of the parishioners leaving says, "I don't care what you say, I still get a creepy feeling when he gives a sermon on brotherly love!"

The Toronto Sun printed a vehement column about gays when it said of the church, "What in the name of sanity has gotten into the Anglican hierarchy? Awhile back they saw spiritual salvation in Mao Tse-tung's totalitarian, robot regime in China—which Mao's successors are now trying to humanize; now, lo, they support black racism and butchery in the name of anti-racism; and now they make a point of approving the ordination of homosexuals as priests. Are they nuts? Why raise the issue at all? Or is this simply another manifestation of the liberal death-wish?"

These are the days when the psychiatric records of clergy gathered at the beginning of a candidate's effort to seek ordination are replete with opinions about the student's psychological makeup, including his or her sexual orientation. Since these records can and sometimes do affect the attitude of those who review them, Bishop Walter D. Dennis submitted to the New York diocesan convention a resolution proposing that "the reports of the psychiatric examinations of candidates for the ministry be destroyed within a reasonable period, not to exceed two years from the ordination of the candidate to the ministry or the withdrawal of his or her application for ordination." If this is in the cause of new freedoms, it is doubtful that it will produce a more healthy effect on the future life of ministers.

Today's approach of screening candidates for the ministry was made fun of in an evaluation letter to "Jesus" regarding his consideration of twelve men selected to join him. It is a typical rebuff to the current selection system.

Mr. J. Christ
12 Lakeview Terrace
Copernawn, Galilee 00666

Dear Mr. Christ:
    We have acted upon your commission to administer a coordinated battery of psychological tests to the twelve candidates whom you are considering as collaborators in an organization you are assembling.

It will be some time before all the data have been processed and interpreted but certain preliminary findings are, in our judgment, of such significance that we are sending them on forthwith.

With regard to Mr. Simon Johnson (or Bar Jona), the profile for this candidate is marked by consistently unsound judgment, excessive emotional reactions, unreliability, and an unrealistic estimate of himself. He tends to be blunt in speech and quite rigid. Luckily you appear to sense this already, as the nickname that you gave him implies. It is our opinion that Johnson, who has been conspicuously unsuccessful as a fisherman and who has had illness in the family, is only speciously magnanimous in his offer to leave all and to follow you. It is accordingly our urgent recommendation that you terminate speedily the association of Johnson with yourself and your organization.

We shall be forwarding further recommendations about the aptitudes of the remaining candidates at an early date. You will want to know that Mr. Thomas Didymus failed to appear for his appointment with our evaluation team. This is usually an indicant of a latent hostility that will impair his usefulness in a corporate effort.

On the evidence assembled thus far we can certainly recommend your associating Mr. J. Iscariot with your enterprise. He has the profile of a completely dependable, hard-working realist. He is open-minded and ready to change. Though he will be a hard-headed, no-nonsense administrator, he has a deep concern for the poor and shows marked potential for growth and advancement in your organization.

In closing, we might note that the mission statement that you submitted to us for your organization, with its description of goals and strategies, struck our staff as incapable of attainment, not to mention verification by the scientific procedures that would make it credible to the world today. Should you, on further consideration, decide to jettison the whole enterprise, we would like to offer you a position on our staff. You have a certain natural flair for dealing with people that, with a few years of professional

formation, ought to be of real service to your fellow
human beings.

Consultation Service Center of
Galilee Tiberiao, Galilee
The Church Advocate, August 1979
Episcopal Diocese of Lexington, Ky.;
(reprinted with permission).

I well remember my own "psychiatric examination." I
had been made a postulant. The first step. But before I could
attend the seminary I was sent to a Dr. Barry. He gave me a
quick Rorschach test. During the test, he told me of a person
who pretended to be epileptic by faking a fit and having soap
in his mouth so he could properly "foam at the mouth." That
was the extent of my test. There was no Commission on
Ministry, nor any further psychological discussions. The concern of the bishop was for my belief in my vocation to the
ministry. Did I feel that Christ was calling me to do his
work? Sex was never mentioned.

Sex is mentioned all the time today. Some church authorities think it always necessary to keep sex in the fore-
front. In England, the Oxford diocesan magazine distributed
in churches had a centerfold with a photo of a nude girl
kneeling. The whole issue was devoted to sex. The editor,
Canon Michael Haytor, commented to reporters: "We've
had nothing but praise for it so far. I hope other churches
will follow our lead." The bishop of Oxford stated: "I really
don't think the magazine will shock people, judging by what
is shown on T.V." So it goes with the British.

The problem with sex is not confined to the homosexual
or lesbian issue; it extends also to married clergy who are
free to divorce and remarry. This issue is very much alive in
Scotland. Professor Thomas Torrance, writing in *Life and
Work,* an official publication of the Church of Scotland, said:
"At no time in my life and ministry have I found or heard of
more cases of marriage breakdown, separation and divorce

and even adultery among those ordained to the holy ministry." Torrance served for one year as moderator of the Church of Scotland. He was in a good position to know the facts.

The study on homosexuality, which was supposed to cause a stir, did not. Masters and Johnson, sex researchers, report a kind of neutral position, having studied ninety-four men and eighty-two women. Whatever the basis of human affection may be, it is not to be learned from sex in the lab.

One of the most sensible statements heard recently is that of Bishop Bennett J. Sims of Atlanta. His view is that we have not dealt with sex as a religious issue. "We fantasize about it, joke, worry, even pray about it. But we are not practiced, most of us, in gathering the whole range of sexual reality into religious reflection. In regard to homosexuality, the most important witness of Scripture is not condemnation, but the promise of liberation." The bishop puts the whole situation in the perspective of our time when he writes: "The wind of a well-intended permissiveness that has sought the release of human creativity has blown us a whirlwind." He sees this era as a crisis of "moral anarchy." [2]

Bishops like Sims have definite views, and they let them be known through speeches and articles. Others ride the trolley of openness. When a bishop of an eastern diocese returned home from the Episcopal General Convention and his clergy read his name on the list of dissenting bishops on the resolution on homosexuality, four of them said, "If that's his attitude, why should we do anything?" The publicity attracted by this group letter at the convention did not detain the bishop from writing a letter the following week asking for money from the diocesan churches for mission work. It did not faze the bishop that what you do can inhibit giving. Money is a weapon in the hands of parishioners. So tense is this issue among other bishops that one such shepherd of the flock demanded all ordinands be required to sign a statement that they were not homosexual. He made this requirement in full vestments just before he began the service of ordination, just before the congregation began the processional hymn. In another diocese, the bishop has a list of "Who's Who" sexually—as well as a list of which priests he hopes will leave the diocese. In England, the then Archbishop Coggan of Canterbury was discovered to have a blacklist, a secret file with marks against names. It was revealed by the Rev. Neil Richardson, vicar of Saint Hugh's, Holts, Oldham. He said, "It leaves no possibility for rehabilitation and, for a church, this is going against the backbone of the Christian faith, which is about forgiveness and new life."

My godly rector told me in my senior year in seminary that one area of my future ministry must be watched very carefully. He referred to sex as an "occupational hazard" of the priesthood. He said, "Bill, it is both a blessing and a curse." He was right, of course. He didn't want me even to have a sofa in my future study or to counsel anyone unless my secretary was in the outer office. "These are ways," he said, "of protecting yourself." Then he explained further: "It isn't always the priest; more often it is the unfulfilled parishioner who sees goodness and wants it!"

In those days there was a sense of discretion in the church. Clergy had problems just like those of the people they were trying to help, but such problems were not out in the open. And with new "freedoms" came new fears. The average parishioner does not appreciate knowing sexual facts about a pastor. So, with all the liberal approaches of today's world, the parish pastor still stands on the brink of tragedy—alone. And sexual indiscretion is still the devil's tool for destroying a parish. A parishioner told me how her sister was shattered by her clergyman's public announcement of his forthcoming divorce and intention of future marriage to a parishioner he was secretly dating. In response to parish chaos he preached a sermon, "Judge Not That Ye Be Not Judged." In earlier days there was an unwritten understanding by both clergy and their supporters that the area of sexual activity was to be handled with the utmost care and good sense because, say what you will, the pastor or priest still remains the Christ-image in the eyes of sensitive Christians. The ministry of the Gospel is still one of the most mysterious of professions. This feeling is captured in a remarkable way in Mary Strong's book, *Letters of the Scattered Brotherhood:*

> As the unseen in you is held captive by the senses so are you a prisoner. The loneliness, the loneliness, the loneliness, which is the lot of all who wonder! Those you see about you are ensnared by the noise, the color, the interests of other souls like yourself; they gather together to do away with this loneliness; all these souls, like yours, are seeking release in affairs in personal experiences; sharing what you call gossip, feelings of patriotism, of endeavor, of art all so far away from the lonely reality of God. It is as if in a multitude of marching men going with one idea to achieve, you turned about right-face and walked back; this is why the road to God is so difficult.[3]

The worldly view of sex is to let it all hang out. That may be liberating for many, but for most individuals sexuality is a latent experience. And laymen see the clergy as sexless. (There comes to mind the bitterness of the phrase, "The clergy is the third sex.") Lay people may fantasize about the clergy, tempt them, think of them as amorous, but in their inmost thoughts they think a man of God can't be a man of sex; yet the history of religion shows that religion in all its aspects is sex oriented. Sex is the *magnum mysterium* of life.

And so we need a captain in life to look to. The priest and pastor is that captain, emulating the role of Christ. As he watches others bear their crosses, so he may bear more than one cross. Blatant or latent? That is the choice for today's clergy, whether married or not.

There is a toll to be paid for being an ambassador for Christ. Clergy are like the musician Franz Liszt. When in the world, they want to be out of it; when out of it, they want to be back in. And the problems of the priest/pastor, whatever they be, even sexual, must be handled alone. They do not consult their bishops for guidance; they should, but they don't: a large segment of the clergy have little or no confidence that bishops or district superintendents or presbytery executives can keep a secret. And the people in the congregations fail to realize that even though the priest/pastor is a symbol for the living ideal of truth, he cannot play the role of perfectionist.

Unlike the Fundamentalist stand, the Anglican approach, for one, has been in the direction of more humanness in personality, thus leaving the door open for error—and open to others as well as the priest/pastor as spiritual director. In Anglicanism, therefore, sex has never been denied—but it also was never proclaimed. Congregations did not overly project the subject of sex to their pastors. But if the pastor became the victim of public scandal or known indiscretion, then it was a different story. Celibacy was not questioned as a possible commitment by a priest; sexual freedom was not in keeping with the idea of true leadership of the church.

Anglican priests were married or unmarried. In either case, they were dedicated to the church. Today's priests, unmarried, are not as frequently considered for a new parish. Yet, as I have stated above, increasing numbers of married priests, and even bishops, are being divorced. It is true that liberalization of sexual restraints has been needed, but this trend among the clergy must be within the context of a gift from God to be wisely used.

To turn to a slightly different perspective on the same subject: In counseling young people, I find that they view sex as much more than an appetite. Their elders would have us believe that all youth are constantly riddled with sexual desire and are about to jump into bed at every opportunity. Not so. Their view is much more spiritual and loving than in the image of sex held of them by adult society. Young people today want sustaining relationships, a sense of peace, security, and enduring relationships. Our society has much more to learn from youth about good sexual ideals than it will learn from the TV talk shows where wealthy showpeople punch out sex innuendoes, bathroom humor, and sickly love talk.

Among the most pervasive of our misapprehensions about sex is our constant use of the word "puritan" to describe all that we think we mean by anti-sex. Our notion of sexual repression seems always couched in terms that are either a defense of or an apology for "puritanism." One of the best correctives to this attitude, and the most helpful in the context of a discussion of the present frenzy in the church, is the article by Leland Ryken that appeared in *The Christian Century* of April 7, 1978. Ryken claims that we have badly misunderstood those old Puritans that we are always admonishing people not to emulate. We say to someone, "Now don't be a Puritan," "I don't want you to think that I'm a Puritan." "I don't like your puritanical attitude."

But, says Leland Ryken, the Puritans saw the sex drive "as created by God, placed it within marriage, enjoyed it, viewed it as the most delicate of all human relationships and one that required personal commitment." But they did not flaunt it in public. They insisted on the privacy of sex because they were certain that sex is sacred, not sinful. Ryken goes on to say that "they knew that a sexual relationship is the least casual and most delicate of relationships—to be entered into with one other person in a situation of deep personal commitment. Unlike the modern tendency to treat sex only as an appetite and to isolate it from the rest of human experience, the Protestant attitude, like the biblical, treats sex as part of a much bigger picture."

It seems to me that the point is that *we* are wrong when we think of the Bible (and the Puritans) as opposed to sex because it has taboos against sexual perversions, including adultery, lechery, homosexuality, and sexual idolatry. The biblical writers were horrified by sexual perversions because they believed sex to be sacred. The Puritans, standing firmly on the Bible, opposed total permissiveness and unrestrained lust. Their ideal of sexual love between husband and wife was a reaction against any negative feeling about sex.

Professor Walter Wink, of Auburn Theological Seminary in New York City, believes that there is no issue more divisive for the churches of America today than the question of ordaining homosexuals. And that issue rests on the question: What does the Bible say about homosexuality, and how are we to apply it to the issue of ordination?

Although it is clear that the Bible takes a negative view of homosexuality, there are other sexual attitudes, practices, and restrictions in the Bible which we no longer accept as normative. (Among those listed by Professor Wink are: the social regulations regarding adultery, incest, rape, and prostitution, which are based on the property rights of males over females; the punishment of adultery by death; polygamy regularly practiced in the Old Testament and, although unmentioned in the New Testament, likely referred to in 1 Timothy 3:2, 12, and Titus 1:6; and levirate marriage and endogamy.)

The problem, as I have said, comes down to our attitude toward the Bible and its authority for us. Dr. Wink speaks for a great many Protestants when he summarizes:

> Clearly we regard certain things, especially in the Old Testament, as no longer binding. Other things we do regard as binding, including legislation in the Old Testament that is not mentioned at all in the New. What is the principle of selection here? Most of us would regard as taboo intercourse with animals, incest, rape, adultery, prostitution, polygamy, levirate marriage and concubinage—even though the Old Testament permits the last four and the New Testament is silent regarding most of them.
>
> How do we make judgments that these should be ta-

boo, however? The problem of authority is not mitigated by the doctrine that the *cultic* requirements of the Old Testament were abrogated by the New, and that only the *moral* commandments of the Old Testament remain in force for Christians. For most of these sexual mores fall among the *moral* commandments . . . The crux of the matter, it seems to me, is simply that the Bible has no sexual ethic. *There is no biblical sexual ethic.* The Bible knows only a love ethic, which is constantly being brought to bear on whatever sexual mores are dominant in any given country, or culture, or period.[4]

Whether one agrees with Dr. Wink's conclusions or not, it seems clear to me that he has correctly identified one of the major components of the present frenzy in the church: the issue of a biblical sexual ethic and its relationship to homosexuality—which is not likely to go away in our lifetime.

In December 1979 the Associated Press reported: "After pondering the subject for five years, the Church of England produced a report today saying that homosexual relationships can be justified and recommending that homosexuals not be barred from the priesthood. But it rejected the concept of marriage between homosexuals. . . . Two bishops involved in preparation of the report clashed over its findings, and the Church's Board for Social Responsibility, which ordered the study, said it was 'deeply divided' over the results."

It appears that Bishop Graham Leonard, the chairman of the Board for Social Responsibility, wrote in a foreword to the report that its members "had not adopted or endorsed the contents." He added, "We do not think the Church of England is yet ready to declare its mind on the subject of homosexuality."

The report itself says that bishops should not refuse to ordain a man merely because he is a homosexual. But it said a homosexual priest living in union with another man should not expect the church to accept him on the same conditions as those of a married priest. Such a priest should offer his resignation, leaving his bishop to decide whether or not to accept it.

The most Reverend Robert Runcie, 102nd archbishop of Canterbury, was later quoted by United Press International as saying that the report is not the church's final word on the subject: "We are still a long way from getting the agreed moral and pastoral guidelines which Church leaders need." And at a press conference in Washington, the retiring archbishop of Canterbury, the Most Reverend F. Donald Coggan, said that it is wrong for a bishop to ordain a man who is a practicing homosexual or a woman who is a practicing lesbian.

Archbishop Coggan's remark offers a quick transition to our next consideration: What about the ordination of women?

Among American denominations, the United Methodist church now has nearly 1,100 ordained women ministers. Of these women, 278 are senior pastors of multiclergy congregations, 197 are pastors, and 41 are associate pastors. The United Methodist church has more women clergy than any other church body.

During the 1979 Diocesan Convention of the Episcopal church in Philadelphia, a priest offered a resolution. He proposed that since the English bishops will not allow American women priestesses to celebrate the Holy Communion, America should retaliate. The English bishops should be informed that no English priest can celebrate the Holy Communion in America.

The resolution was shouted down, but the frustration of some clergy is still apparent in a church where the ordination of women has become a very divisive problem. (Another priest, in trying to propose a dental and medical health plan, finally ended by calling it a mental plan. The bishop agreed that indeed the Episcopal church may need a mental plan for the goodly number of clergy who are still in a frenzy over women priests.)

Within the human sexuality issue and as part of the male-female identity problem, dioceses created their study committees on the subject of women priests. They divided into camps that took on all of the aspects of the issue: theological, psychological, practical, sociological, ecumenical, and historical. But even without these study groups, the die was cast for ordination. Militants were already at work in the effort to convince and to act.

Not only was Christianity in the throes of the feminine upheaval, so also was Judaism. Jews had their first female rabbi in 1972, Rabbi Sally Priesand. And, of course, feelings in the Roman Catholic church are demonstrated by the challenge to authority made by Sister Theresa Kane during the pope's visit to the United States in October of 1979. She did what no other nun had dared to do. She stood up in the grandeur of the National Shrine of the Immaculate Conception in Washington on the last day of Pope John Paul's tour, and said: "I *urge* you, Your Holiness, to be open and to respond to the voices coming from the women of this country who are desirous of serving in and through the church as *fully* participating members."

And after that speech, Sister Margaret Ellen Traxler of Chicago called Sister Theresa a modern Joan of Arc.

Pope John Paul II does not believe in the ordination of women. He never will. Even Pope Paul VI said that the ordination of women was "not in accordance with God's plan for His church." (The presiding bishop of the Episcopal church said: "Women can no more be priests than they can become fathers or husbands.") As in the long-ago march for women's suffrage, some four thousand women marched in Baltimore in November 1978, demanding that women be ordained in the Roman Catholic church. Their banners proclaimed, "Rites Are Our Right." The procession was six blocks long.

Compounding the issue is Dr. Dorothy Irvin. She claims the missing link is in the slides and lectures she presents claiming to prove the existence of women priests and bishops in the early Church. As an archaeologist on the theology faculty, College of Saint Catherine in Saint Paul, Minnesota, her photos of ancient mosaics and frescoes are causing a stir. It is not known if the figures could be merely deaconesses and abbesses. They did exist.

As far back as 1976, Paul VI told the archbishop of Canterbury that "grave difficulty" would arise regarding the dialogue between Roman Catholics and Anglicans on the question of women's ordination. Nothing has happened since then to change that conviction. But parish priests and parish churchwomen will not be easily dissuaded.

Outside the mainline denominations the problem is no less acute. Mormon women were allowed to give prayers in church meetings, but this was only a small step toward ordination because, the hierarchy said, "It is an essential part of Mormon doctrine that only faithful males hold the priesthood and perform its ordinances, including baptism, confirmation and marriage." The Swedish Lutheran Church collapsed on the issue of ordination of women, according to an essay in the book *Man, Woman, Priesthood*, published in the United States by Christian Classics.

The Church of England was seriously divided when the Lambeth Conference decision in 1978 approved the ordination of women, but then voted not to carry it through when the General Synod, the ruling body, met and changed its mind. A woman, Una Knoll, told them off. She shouted at the assembled delegates, "We asked you for bread and you gave us a stone. Long live God!" The bishops were for it. The laymen were for it. But the clergy were against it.

Pope John Paul II told Anglican leaders in 1978 that

"Our haste to achieve unity, the urgency of putting to an end the intolerance of scandal of division among Christians, obliges us to avoid all imprudence." The ordination issue did not further that plea for unity. Nor will it in the future.

William Stringfellow, a lawyer-author who is called an "Episcopal lay theologian," made a speech to the Religion Newswriters Association at the 1979 Episcopal General Convention. In it he called for the resignation of Presiding Bishop John Allin. Among other things, Stringfellow accused Allin of incompetent leadership, of managing the church instead of directing it, of being insensitive to the issue of tax privileges, and of being unable to listen to criticism of church investments. Then Stringfellow hit Allin with the big arrow: Allin's stand against ordaining women.

As presiding bishop, Allin was relatively immune to criticism. The lower ranks of clergy are not so fortunate. One bishop made it clear to his clergy that if a priest did not approve of the ordination of women, he was not welcome in the bishop's diocese. In the United Presbyterian church's New York Presbytery, two candidates for the ministry were refused permission to work in local churches because they did not believe in the ordination of women.

In 1979, Rev. Allison Cheek said: "Women priests are supplying something which has been missing in a lopsided church." The priestess problem prompted publishers to go after stories about women priests. Harper & Row published *A Priest Forever,* the story of Rev. Carter Heyward, one of the eleven women ordained in the illegal ordination by the Episcopal bishops in Philadelphia on July 29, 1974. Whether the illegal (now called "irregular") ordinations are truly illegal is a subject that still irks and confounds clergy cocktail parties and bull sessions.

But the real wing-ding, shotgun blast at the church occurred when the bishop of New York ordained an avowed lesbian. In his book *Take A Bishop Like Me,* Bishop Paul Moore defended his action. Others said that he "betrayed the trust the church has given him . . . what right has he to inflict so much pain on others?"

The feeling that pain had been caused parishioners by the actions of bishops and clergy is widespread throughout all the denominations. *The Presbyterian Layman,* an unofficial publication issued by Presbyterian dissidents, always has a "letters to the editor" column in which expressions of pain are the chief theme.

An Episcopalian physician wrote to his rector to express his own pain at the actions of his church: "Why should I contribute to a church I have loved and honored when bishops make a fool of me?"

A general disregard for others seems apparent in the actions of many church leaders who make public statements that blatantly deny what they have been charged to uphold. Lord Fisher, a former archbishop of Canterbury, issued a statement in 1971 that quickly made all the papers. The Associated Press carried the story here in the United States, quoting him as saying that "sexual intercourse between engaged couples would not be regarded in the moral sense as fornication." He would permit young unmarried couples to sleep together with the church's blessing. (At the time Fisher made the statement, he was eighty-three years old.)

A different kind of pain, occasioned by the problem of ordained women, resulted when it became apparent that the eleven original ordinands of the Episcopal church had not been able to assume the expected roles. Allison Cheek became a psychotherapist; Carter Heyward an assistant professor of theology at the Episcopal Seminary in Cambridge, Massachusetts; Nancy Wittig had no formal post; Betty Schiess became a chaplain at Syracuse University; Suzanne Hiatt became associate professor of pastoral theology at the now defunct Philadelphia Divinity School; Merrill Bittner just stepped out, although she is still a priestess; Jeanette Piccard, now eighty-five, is resting.

The attempt to suspend the bishops for their part in

those original ordinations came to nothing. Presentments against them amounted only to a heavy exchange of letters designed to establish the positions of the writers. It was a frenzy among the bishops.

The Right Reverend Albert A. Chambers, one of the four bishops in the "irregular" ordination of the eleven women, wrote Presiding Bishop John Allin a "Dear John" letter in July, 1978: "When I was consecrated I did take an oath to 'conform to the doctrine, discipline, and worship of the Protestant Episcopal Church in the United States of America,' and I had always done that. But the House of Bishops, including those who now charge me with a breach of the Constitution and Canons, have themselves so emasculated the doctrine of the Church and vulgarized and degraded its worship that it is not recognizable as the doctrine and worship that I pledged and still pledge myself to uphold."

The bishops not only caused much pain between themselves, they also left in the wake of their rancorous debates on the subject a large group of women who were calling the bishops "sexists" and accusing them of "male arrogance." The pain reached such a fever point that Betty Bone Schiess initiated a suit against the bishop who did not recognize her ordination, the Right Reverend Ned Cole of Central New York. The suit was later withdrawn, but not before she had accused the bishop of violating her rights because of her sex and of conspiring with other bishops to violate her priesthood.

The pain of the frenzy surfaced again during the trial of Rev. William Wendt, rector of Saint Stephen and the Incarnation Church of Washington. It was almost like a Perry Mason thriller. Father Wendt allowed one of the "Philadelphia Eleven" women priests to celebrate Holy Communion in his church. At the trial that followed there was a great deal of arguing over the meaning of such phrases as "godly admonition," of Wendt's "alleged" disobedience and, of course, Allison Cheek's ordination.

In his own defense, Father Wendt said, "My conscience was informed through Scripture. Jesus spoke against the legalists of his own time. He also spoke out for women, which was a revolutionary stance for those times."

After all the fireworks, Father Wendt carried on as rector and Allison Cheek's name is still listed on page 110 of the Episcopal Clerical Directory. She is assistant at Saint Stephen and the Incarnation Church.

But the pain had spread far afield. Dissension appeared at Christ Cathedral, Montreal. Twenty-six clergy and fifty lay people walked out on the ordination of Lettie James. In spite of this, reports of the event said that "she was bursting with joy." She felt that the protesters were within their own rights and, being the first woman priest in that diocese, she understood their protest.

Canon Susan Klein of Christ Church Cathedral in St. Louis, Missouri, wrote to *The Witness* (Jan. 1980) and said that "Mary was the first priest because she was the first person to bring Christ into the world." Also that Mary was the "real symbol of revolutionary power . . . . a powerful revolutionary Mother. What the church really needs is fewer sermons on 'Mommyology' and a greater number that glorify revolutionary motherhood, Mary as mother of liberation, true head of the movement to free the oppressed, and as the first priest." She then slapped it on her readers by asking, "Are you ready to bear Christ in YOUR wombs?"

In all this frenzy about women pastors and priests, the common theme seems to be that God has gone feminine. In the belief that we need more She than He, two Jewish women have created a Jewish Sabbath prayer book. Maggie Wenig and Naomi Janowitz like the phrases, "Shelter us in the soft folds of your skirt," and, "She soothes those in pain and cradles the abandoned." They believe strongly that women need to know that they are also created in the image of God. Aggressive women who seek ordination don't want to hear about maleness, only about humanness. If they are Christian women, they want an androgynous Christ. Even so, there seems to be a hidden apathy (perhaps a psychologist would call it "repressed hostility") toward women priests. This is often evident at assembly meetings of denominational delegates. When several women pastors or priests appear for a two-day conference, usually dominated by males, they are not the center of attention. If the convention consists of, say, 250 priests and only a handful of priestesses, very few of the men gravitate to the females. Sometimes they are turned off by such remarks as, "Hi! I'm the new den mother of the Church of The Advocate."

At Westminster Abbey, I attended Evensong. The procession included a male choir, the dean and his staff. Leading the procession was a woman verger. An American tourist near me remarked to his wife, in all sincerity, "Is she the choir mother?" Perhaps the woman verger was the Anglican way of saying, "We're going along with this, but not all the way."

In a diocese neighboring mine, women priests did assist at the convention Eucharist by administering the chalices. But the tension was high among the clergy who still were not convinced that women should be ordained. One male chalice-bearer tried to head for the priests that he knew didn't want to receive from women priests. Glares and frozen stares went back and forth. One woman priest had not left her Communion station in time to be handed her chalice. She tried to open the altar rail several times. She was told to go around through the sacristy. But she kept repeating, "I've got to get in there and get that chalice." In the sacristy after the service there was a gallon of wine overconsecrated. It was a woman priest who looked at it, laughed, and said, "Boy, look at what we have to drink!"

There seems no end to the effort to justify the ordination

of women. As a parish priest, I have my own feelings about the issue of women's liberation and rights. This is a theological issue that reflects the very nature of Christ. And it is an issue that does not resolve itself through the argument that Jesus chose men as his disciples because they were the only people available, or because women were of less stature in those days.

God is focused in Christ, like sun through a glass, creating power. Christ embodies the divine attributes: goodness, mercy, truth, forgiveness, understanding, and strength. What we see in Jesus are the qualities of an ideal parent; He relates to us in the universal concept of a Heavenly Father. God is a Father. Jesus is a Son.

Yes, there is humanness. But there is also maleness. He is a He, make no mistake about it. The qualities that Jesus presents for us are for both male and female. Yet there is a certain something that is inherent in the male that distinguishes him as a leader. The male commands and directs, but with gentle firmness. This is a mystical concept and not at all relevant to the contemporary discussion of male-female identity roles. The female is ideally seen in the role that Mary portrayed. In it the woman is not subservient or less a person; there is more of beauty and sustaining comfort. She is supportive but not dominant. The line is drawn between the sexes. Each has its own drama to unfold. "Mother, behold thy son. Son, behold thy mother." These insights seem to me to be universal teachings.

The question remains: Can a woman be ordained? Yes. Can she be a priest in terms of a theological or mystical truth? No.

No matter what the traditional denomination procedures may be, a church subjected to a democratic process in the guise of "new freedoms" and "the elimination of sexist inequality" will emerge with a structure where the mystery once represented is overshadowed. It will, in the end, be a church that marches off to join a super pan-protestantism.

There are problems that the fringe groups of Protestantism do not have to face. But the mainstream churches do face them. Christian Science has its women practitioners, Spiritualism has women ministers, but Roman Catholics, Anglicans, Greek Orthodox, and Russian Orthodox leaders must make a decision. It is now after the fact in the Episcopal, Methodist, Presbyterian, and other major denominations. Ordination of women has already happened and, take it or leave it, there are women clergy. (One vestryman, and he is not alone, agreed that there should be women priests—but he would not hire one.)

I would not be honest with my reader if I did not write that I find the voted changes in Episcopal canon law regarding the ordination of women totally unacceptable. Having dedicated my life to the church and ministered in churches for over twenty-three years, not including my youth, my feelings are not based on mere opinion. I believe that the Episcopal church has made a great—and historic—error. Worse yet, it has made a grave theological error. It can never be corrected. Further, I believe that the actions of the various conventions of the Episcopal church that led to this change in its canon law cannot be attributed to the action of the Holy Spirit.

The Episcopal church has reaped the results of the relentless work of militant and radical liberals who have used parliamentary maneuvers and politics zealously to bring about their intended goals. These goals were originally presented in the supposed interest of "renewal." But those in the episcopate who insisted on the ordination of women have now distorted the very mysteries that they are commissioned to protect. Indeed, they have placed in jeopardy the entire teaching of the sacramental life of the church.

The thirty-seven bishops who would not subscribe to the original ordinations of the women are now silent. Bishop Dmitri, a spokesman for the Orthodox church, said, "I do not think a Convention has the right to make such a change.

To subject a tradition of the church to a democratic process is wrong. It is as if you changed the Sabbath to Tuesday. We have a tradition inherited from New Testament times that gives us no warrant for changing the Sabbath or for ordaining women."

Some congregations couldn't care less, but those who labor in the "carhop" parish ministry day and night live a tense and often hectic emotional life. We move daily from birth to death, and we encounter all the problems of life in between. We also juggle countless facets of parish activities— from the demands of creative written material for the public to the manifold administration obligations and the pressure of financial concerns at home as well as at the church. We are not admitted to the decision-making levels of our national church. That function is left to those who are not parochially oriented and, indeed, have little or no recent practical parish experience.

In all my years as a priest I have never encountered more demoralized clergymen than I do today. These clergy have not lost their faith, but they have watched the framework around it begin to come apart in an alarming fashion.

It is at this point of the shaking of the foundations of faith that what I have called the "frenzy in the church" has spread across all the branches of Christendom today. Laity as well as clergy in all portions of the worldwide community of Christians have found themselves caught up in a misguided effort to impose drastic changes on a two-thousand-year-old tradition—all in the name of a fleeting, so-called "demand of our culture."

The peace of the church is at stake.

CHAPTER FOUR

PRAISE THE LORD

Praise the Lord! I heard that phrase shouted over and over again as I stood outside a storefront church in Highlands, New Jersey, when I was a child. As I peered in through the screen door of the small building next to the A&P, I saw people rolling on the floor, shrieking, waving their hands, and trembling. It frightened me, especially when my mother told me that they were "Holy Rollers." I didn't know what that meant, but it was my first encounter with the Pentecostalists.

Living near Asbury Park, I often watched the preachers in the great auditorium at Ocean Grove. I remember those preachers pounding the pulpit and issuing stern "altar calls." I was fascinated, but even though it was clear to me that they were more zealous (and louder) than the preacher in my own church, I was never drawn to their style of expression in worship.

When I went to seminary, I was able to observe such preachers as Oral Roberts in his Tent Healing Ministry and A. A. Allen at the old Philadelphia Met with his miracle revivals. Allen was an especially aggressive personality, flamboyant and persuasive. He claimed to heal people and to exorcise their demons into mason jars right in front of a jam-packed auditorium. The force and the drive of these preachers was not only theatrical, it was also hysterical. They were the "Spirit-filled," "born-again" Christians whose interpretation of the Bible was firm and unequivocal. They preached the Word of God in a slam-bang, sock-it-to-you style that could curl your hair, make your knees knock, and dangle you over the flaming pits of Hell. They were the Pentecostals, the Charismatics of their day. And their preachers were not so much mysterious to me as they were perplexing and unsettling. It was "straight Bible talk," and every listener was sure that these men could not go wrong.

Those preachers felt that the Holy Spirit could knock you out of your seat with a heaven-sent power, and in the midst of that knocking you would be born again. Born of the Spirit. A road-to-Damascus experience all your own. From that point on your life would be different. It said so in the Bible. And, of course, their interpretation of the Bible did not have to be loaded down with scholarly details. What the Bible said, it said. "If the Bible says it, I believe it. And that's the end of it."

And if the Bible said that people spoke "in tongues," then it was clear that people were meant to speak in tongues. So they did. Some people thought that speaking in tongues was reserved for a special kind of Christian.

But speaking in tongues is not unusual today. A great many Christians across the United States and in all parts of the world have embraced what they once rejected: the religious experience of the storefront Christians. That religious experience is held to be a Spirit-filled, emotional release from the tensions and hangups of contemporary living. The emphasis on experience is often held to be the direct antithesis of a rigorous and rational understanding of the doctrines of the Christian faith. Thus inhibitions that once could not be released in public are now set free in the charismatic worship service. But to my mind, whether all this is truly of the Holy Spirit is a big question. Churches in which people once sat or kneeled quietly in prayer are now bubbling cauldrons of wild-eyed expression.

In these churches, which have opened themselves to the charismatic experience, clergy who were supposed to have been born again at their baptism have now been "baptized with the Holy Spirit and with fire." One rector became so fired up that he began to preach tirades against his own congregation, to convince them that they were not Christians! His people, faithful to their Lord for many years, were told that they had never found Christ. Finally, the congregation was so divided that the rector was forced to resign. He moved on to another church and repeated the same process. On being asked at that church if he could shorten his forty-five-minute sermons, he replied, "Do you really expect me to tell the Spirit to stop?"

At the time of this writing, the 1979 Youth Conference of the Episcopal Diocese of New Jersey had a theme of "Dancing and Leaping and Praising God." It was a celebration of the joy of the Christian life, in which each participant was to bring his own instrument to "provide a joyful noise at the Eucharist." It is this kind of indoctrination into Charismatic and Fundamentalist religion that has now made inroads into every major denomination. A "carried-away" atmosphere now appears necessary in almost every church service in order to make it an "authentic experience of worship."

"Do you go to church?" I asked an acquaintance of mine. "Yes," he replied, "but I don't know what to expect each time I go!"

That attitude is characteristic of many worshipers today. The changes have come so thick and fast and are of such a depth that parishioners, especially older ones, are feeling as if they are adrift at sea in an open boat. Perhaps there is, indeed, a need to let people know that Christians are not sad people, solemn and glum all the time. But in trying to counteract that notion, the church has slipped into exhibitionism. Even if these "experiences" are Spirit-inspired, which I personally doubt, they are still exhibitionistic.

When the newspapers reported that thirty-one bishops, in full ecclesiastical vestments, danced around the altar at Canterbury Cathedral at the 1978 Lambeth Conference, a friend remarked to me, "Did they do the Lambeth Two-step?"

Yes, one can support charismatic behavior by scripture. It is nothing new. But it does require interpretation. Actually, it is the old Pentecostalism in modern dress. And the church has bought it in the belief that it is the Holy Spirit renewing everything in the church.

About all this, Cardinal Leo J. Suenens said, "I feel that the future of the charismatic renewal, which is chiefly a move of the Spirit within the church rather than a movement, is to disappear into the bloodstream of the Body of Christ. The charismatic renewal is the Holy Spirit working in the church, filling it with fresh air, renewing it."

Part of that may be true, but I, for one, do not think that it is renewing the church. In many instances, it has divided the church by producing two distinct groups within it. Those who have been "filled" are in one group. Those who have not been "filled" are told that they must be "filled" before they can truly meet Jesus. In some congregations, baptism of the Holy Spirit as an "experience" (sometimes evidenced by the ability to speak in tongues) has become a requirement; indeed, in many churches it has become the only requirement. In other words, whatever the Christian's experience has been, it has not been enough. A recent born-again charismatic clergyman asked his organist of fourteen years if *he* was "born again." The organist said, "I think I am." The next day he fired him.

But I protest. Although we must indeed be "born again"—and countless Christians know that they have been—

such rebirth does not have to be in the mode and manner of the charismatics.

In respect to the Roman Catholic church, the Most Reverend Robert J. Dwyer of Portland, Oregon, said of Pentecostalism: "It does not need the Church . . . her authority . . . her sacraments." In other words, according to the Pentecostals, if you are baptized by the Spirit, you don't need water baptism, confirmation, and the strengthening gifts of the Holy Spirit. You have it. The archbishop also commented: "If, in addition, the gift of tongues is super-added, there is no further need for the preaching and catechesis of the Church. It may be gibberish, but it is held to be the ultimate of divine communication." [1]

The Lutheran Medical Center of Brooklyn conducted a study on glossolalia. The researchers used psychological testing, personal interviews, and tape recordings of services and meetings where people purportedly spoke in languages they had never studied and did not understand. Apart from feelings of peace and inspiration, they found that certain types of personalities who experience such phenomena are those who have submissive relationships to authority. In other words, the charismatic type is an individual who can submit to someone or something other than himself or herself. Such people have something within them that causes them to give themselves totally to a leader. We have seen this in its most devastating expression in the allegiance with which his followers gave themselves to Rev. Jim Jones in Guyana.

Speaking in tongues, and other evidences of the charismatic experience, seem to require a definite kind of emotional content in the personality of the individual. The Charismatics themselves say that this is the result of a direct divine intervention in their lives. While I believe that such divine intervention can and does take place, I think that this is not true in every case of glossolalia. I am also very much aware that the sweep of the so-called "Spirit-filled" religion is spreading like wildfire through both organized and unorganized religion. From the Jesus People to Roman Catholic Pentecostals to mainline Episcopalians and to the rebirth of Fundamentalist radio and television religion, there is evidence on every side of spirit-drenched charismatics.

When the controversial James Pike was the Episcopal bishop of California, he established a Study Commission on Glossolalia within his diocesan Division of Pastoral Services. Whatever evaluation of Bishop Pike one may make (and he may even be considered tame today), it is true that he did a remarkable job in handling a problem that eventually permeated the whole fabric of parishes and missions throughout the land. The fact that his personal life became a human tragedy in no way diminishes the value of the report that his commission prepared, or of his subsequent pastoral letter to his clergy about the whole matter of speaking in tongues.

The report of Bishop Pike's study commission reviewed the beginnings of tongue-speaking in 1958 at Holy Spirit Episcopal Church, Monterey Park, California; at Trinity Episcopal Church, Wheaton, Illinois; and at the well-known Saint Mark's Episcopal Church, Van Nuys, California, where the rector later resigned because of the controversy. In 1963, there were about twelve clergy and two hundred laity involved in the California experience. And in the Pike Report there were many references to the mechanics of surrender, release, power, transformation, and joy. The report also included an account of what the tongues sounded like:

What does tongues sound like? Again, two kinds must be distinguished. Most common is a "lalling" in a tongue without human counterpart. It usually has a more or less developed phonic structure, as might be expected. According to those who use tongues, as one becomes more practiced in its use, the "language" becomes more fluent. It stresses open vowels and a general lack of harsh gutterals, somewhat in the manner of Hawaiian or a southern Romance language. The other kind is more rare, but that which receives the greater publicity; namely, the use by a person of a human language which he has not studied and could not "possibly" have learned. The literature abounds with examples where this is reported to have taken place.[2]

The section of Bishop Pike's pastoral letter that deals with the psychological aspects of tongue-speaking is very important today in light of the widespread use of the term "Holy Spirit" to describe current experiences reported by both young and old people. Many of these people have left their own churches to follow the path of what Dr. Marcus Bach called "the Inner Ecstasy." These followers believe that such a path will lead them more quickly toward their goal of a "Bible-centered religion," a goal of which they had despaired in their established churches.

Interestingly, the Pike report points out that "Glossolalia is not *per se* a religious phenomenon. In its non-religious manifestations, it appears among adults who are suffering from mental disorders such as schizophrenia and hysteria. It is not necessarily healthy or wholesome in a given person's life. Its goodness or badness depends upon ability to harmonize it with other experience. Self-control must be a factor."

The report also covered autosuggestion, which can be stimulated by repeating such phrases as "Jesus, Jesus, Jesus" or "Heal, Heal, Heal, Heal." The authors of the report spoke of spirit possession as, in some cases, the possibility that the voice or the language came from a demon. This reminds us that the phenomenon is not Christian in origin. References to it are found in the ancient mystery religions and in Egyptian writers. Devotees of these religions were all possessed of something. And that something is the question. How that something works is the problem. It was a question and a problem thousands of years ago, and it is so today.

The scope of the present Charismatic movement may be

seen in a report filed by George W. Cornell, religion editor for the Associated Press. Appearing as a syndicated column in newspapers across the country, Cornell's report described the assembly called "Jesus '79." This was really a series of rallies involving Evangelicals, Protestants, and Roman Catholics. In 1978, over sixty thousand persons gathered in Giants Stadium in New Jersey for a day-long celebration of singing, praying, swaying, preaching, cheering, and chanting—all to proclaim that Jesus 's Lord.

On Saturday, June 2, 1979, there were twenty-seven such gatherings in the United States and in twenty overseas cities such as Belfast, Dublin, Bombay, and Algiers. The Reverend Dr. Vincent Synan, organizer of the Oklahoma City rally and secretary of the Pentecostal Holiness Church, looks for this movement to produce a new level of Christian unity. "The infectious joy of the Holy Spirit would then flow back into the churches and bless them," he said.

But in the September 1979 issue of the *Parish News/ Trends Letter,* both Roman Catholics and Lutherans were reported to be asking themselves the question: "Has the charismatic movement already peaked?" Whatever the reason, the most recent statistics seem to show clearly that in terms of total numbers involved, the movement is at a plateau. Nevertheless, the history of the Christian Church offers convincing proof that this is a recurring phenomenon among people of all shades of Christian belief. I am sure that we will have the charismatic experience with us at one level or another in the decades ahead.

It seems to me that, as indicated in Bishop Pike's pastoral letter, we would do well to consider both the cultural and psychological factors that are at work in those who are strongly attracted by the charismatic "gifts." One of the most important cultural factors is the widespread acceptance among both young people and adults of the notion that "feeling" is somehow more authoritative than "intellect." It should be immediately evident that we have endured a period of anti-intellectualism in this country, if not throughout the world, during the past twenty years. Somehow it has become more important for people to know *how they feel* than to know *what to think*. And it is this line of "reasoning" that has played a great part in the resurgence of the Charismatic movement. (It also appears to be the foundation on which most of the cults are built.) Thus the two-thousand-year-old tradition of carefully thought out doctrines of theology and liturgy, upon which the mainstream of both Protestant and Roman Catholic faith is built, is not being tossed aside as lacking in authority—because it does not "feel" right. What a tragedy that God's gift of thousands and thousands of the finest minds in human history have been so carelessly cast away!

Another cultural factor that must be considered in any effort to understand the attraction of the Charismatics is the mood of relativity that is abroad in the land today. Almost everything about our life today, to many people, seems to be unstable. Someone has said that "it is as if we were floating on an open sea of uncertainty with nothing to guide us, nothing to give us direction, nothing to assure us that we are going in the right direction toward a secure tomorrow."

I know many people who would agree that such a statement represents their own situation. And, indeed, in a time when it seems easily possible to line up an equal number of reputable authorities on either side of almost any question, such uncertainty and insecurity almost guarantee that people will be looking for something that is "sure." And if the Charismatic groups can produce a "feeling" of assurance, they will always find new members. But I have serious doubts that this kind of assurance is true to the Bible, or to the long tradition of the Christian faith.

CHAPTER FIVE

WORSHIP THE LORD

I believe that the phrase "Praise the Lord" does not necessarily include the same content of meaning that surrounds the phrase "Worship the Lord." If, in the last chapter, we examined the charismatic aspects of the former phrase, let us now look at what is happening to some of the more staid characteristics of the latter phrase.

Attending a service of worship can be a disquieting experience or one of peace and healing. Hypertense clergy tend to conduct hyperservices, while more sedate and calm clergy project a quiet atmosphere of worship. A great deal depends upon their varying ability to speak well and project the voice properly. As a member of The Players, a theatrical club in New York City, I had occasion to meet a number of professional actors. One man, who had played in Shakespearean drama, said to me, "I think it would do the clergy well to spend time in summer theatre, where they could get used to being in front of people as part of their field training. As it is, they can't read aloud too well and their emphasis is all misplaced. With this new prayer book in your church, and its small-town language, I doubt that even an actor could deliver convincingly." Then he added, "I should know. I'm an actor and I've been a churchman for years."

The manner in which the Episcopal church has conducted worship services for many, many years has been enhanced by the very language of the prayer book. The same has been true of both the United Presbyterian church and the Presbyterian church in the United States. Even if the priest or the pastor was not able to speak very well, at least the printed words made up for his fault. Now, with the new revisions in the stately prayer books, things have changed indeed.

As is well known, the British are much better at conducting services and ceremonials than are the Americans. Their use of the English language, their pace, their delivery, and even the gothic settings of their sanctuaries create a mood that many American clergy run home to when they travel to England, Scotland, and Wales.

"Things haven't changed much at Westminster Abbey," said a rector who returned from England. He was speaking of the funeral of Lord Louis Mountbatten, where none of the "modern" liturgical forms were in evidence. The state trumpets, the great organ, the men and boy's choir—all seemed to him to be the height of dignity in an age of religious frivolity. Yet he also said that in the smaller villages of England and Wales much "reform" has taken place. And the experimentation in worship is not always to the liking of small-town congregations.

Traveling churchmen are a good barometer of trends in worship. One couple recently told me that they attended a Holy Communion service in an Episcopal church in Florida. The service was over in twenty minutes. The clergyman raced through the prayers, did not greet the people afterward, and not one parishioner spoke to the couple. At another service there were so many people doing so many things in an effort to provide "something for everyone" that the whole service was like the performance of a Broadway show. In still another, so much mimeographed material was distributed to the worshipers that the sanctuary was strewn with paper as the service ended. My friend remarked, "This place looks like the floor of the Stock Exchange."

In another church, the Exchange of Peace was exuberant enough to make a person think that he was a guest on "Love Boat." One pastor was heard to exclaim about the liturgical guidelines sent to him from diocesan headquarters: "My God, I'll need a professional choreographer to set this up!"

A woman reported that her pastor had gone on a study leave to England and returned to his pulpit with a British accent. "He suddenly wanted to have tea with everyone and he began to wear his cassock downtown to the supermarket," she said. Another clergyman topped his colleague by appearing in the doorway after a funeral wearing his black cape. "That was normal," said the local funeral director, "but the derby hat and umbrella on his arm make him look like a character from Monty Python."

Behavior in Episcopal churches has always engendered a variety of responses. Unlike those Protestants who sit for worship, the Church of England does have a liturgy, a form of worship, a prescribed way of doing it. A parishioner once described it as the "up and down church." People do not merely sit and watch, listening to four anthems sung by the choir and a long sermon. Instead, they participate. The genius of the Book of Common Prayer is its plan for the involvement of people in a corporate act of worship in common with God and man.

The criticism of the Episcopal service has been that we did it the same way all the time. But that criticism is no longer valid. The once visible unity of the church, which was cemented by the Book of Common Prayer, has crumbled. Episcopal churches are all doing different things now.

One service of worship that set apart the Episcopal church was the Eucharist. In that service there was a mystery and a oneness that not only brought to mind what happened on the final night of Jesus' life, but enacted it in a manner and mood that conformed to the teaching and belief in the presence of Christ. That manner and mood has changed.

If I remember anything churchly from my youth, it is the vicar in our small Saint Andrew's, Highlands, New Jersey, mission driving a great distance to celebrate reverently the Holy Communion. That service was a quiet and solemn time in my formative years. I knew that something important was happening, something that was mysterious beyond reason. I remember that I would look up at Father Grimshaw or Father Snyder as the bread was blessed and the chalice lifted. Before me was a peaceful man standing at the altar as I knelt to receive the Bread of Life. (I certainly could not imagine a clapping, dancing, or yelling church then.) It was a Presence that both the priest and I acknowledged. And perhaps what I sensed was also a balance, a right attitude, and a man properly dressed for the occasion.

There were no great gothic arches to inspire me, no long aisle of red carpet—and no upbeat group waiting for the next friendly trip to a ball game. It was a small congregation in a town with many saloons. We lived upstairs over my uncle's tavern. But in that small church I received a sense of God's presence and some esthetic insight. There were no jazz masses, rock groups, or tape decks. There wasn't even a pipe organ, just a small, one-manual early-model electric organ played by Ruth Lucas.

In that little church during worship services there was a sense of the *mysterium tremendum*. There can be simplicity in mystery. The Episcopal church once had it. I say "once" because a certain something has slowly eroded the masterpiece of the Anglican church and, indeed, the other denominations. Although still impressive, current worship services are often very much stripped of mystery.

The need for mystery is an internal longing. This is evidenced by the continued interest by the general public in such topics as ESP and the allied psychic subjects, not to mention the ongoing fascination with Eastern religions. In *Worship,* one of the most influential books of our time, the great Anglican scholar of the spiritual life, Evelyn Underhill, wrote that "worship is a supernatural action; and more than a supernatural action, a supernatural life." I believe that. As Canon Robert J. Lewis said of Evelyn Underhill, "Her gift was to reach minds struggling towards enlightenment. Her unique ability was to guide souls into a 'sense of God.' " She once wrote to a friend, "Things are moving in the supernatural world. Don't you feel this—in spite of all that seems so hostile to religion?"

I, too, believe that things are moving in the supernatural world. I believe that God will ultimately get his way, no matter what the patterns of modern religion create. If we believe that God is the Supreme Ruler of all that is, then he will work out the salvation of his people—with or without the structures we have known and worked with in the past. This is why, in updating what is sacred, the ways of man are not always the ways of God.

Certainly worship is more than Sunday and more than an everyday recognition of what appears to be holy. This is why a sense of mystery is important to religion and to the church. This is the basic theme of the Eucharist, which lifts the people beyond the mere fellowship meal to a spiritual banquet—not a picnic. To secularize the Eucharist is to bring worship to a horizontal level rather than to its exalted vertical position.

There is a type of "worship" that is not worship. The participants do not want the mystery. They want a celebration: a celebration of life. But since the pagans celebrated life, what is it that Christians should celebrate? They celebrate the Resurrection of Christ. They celebrate the open doors of death. And they celebrate the life to come which is with us now. There is joy, but also solemnity. There is mystery because we deal with the unknown. There is awe because we take our places for a mystery meal, an encounter with the supernormal in bread and wine. Why should language become less special, more common? God deserves the best. If God deserves the best in a house of worship built of stone by people providing the best stained glass, the best bell they can afford, the best organ—then why should not the manner of worship and the language be the best?

But instead of the best language, words can become less dignified, alternative ways of worship become simply variety, and God becomes more depersonalized. Also, those who are "less restricted" can feel the pulse of a new super-church, a hopeful, ecumenical over-church made up of all the churches rather than a selection of pathways to the Ultimate. This type of change easily brings a loss of the sacred in many of the individual traditions. In the midst of secular paranormal interest, the paranormal life of the church is thinned out very drastically.

The worship services of the church are also affected by a new kind of pastor, the one who is looking for the action somewhere else. When I prepared for the ministry there were special ministries, to be sure, but the seminary was chiefly concerned with the ongoing life of the parish. In recent years the concern has been for the "outside" ministries. Even so, perhaps we shall see a return to the parish ministry, where there is action on every level of involvement with pastoral concerns. The call of the work of Christ requires all types of people. The ministries of social action, the attempts to change society, the missions to every conceivable area of life, have extended the influence of the church beyond anything known in earlier times. The old idea of mission was that you brought people to Christ. The new thinking of mission includes any social cause that one chooses. Talking about Christ is optional.

Even though the accomplishments of these special ministries have improved life on some levels, they have not engendered a sense of worship or a consciousness-raising
experience. Since the early days of Christianity, worship has
been a central part of the life and effort of the church. I once
thought it humorous when the Galilee Mission in Philadelphia required the derelicts on old Race Street to sit
through a talk or sermon in a worship service before giving
them a free meal. As a young man, I thought, "Why don't
they just feed them? Why force them to sit through a prayer
service?" Now I can understand. Yes, the churches should
help to feed the world's hungry, demanding nothing in return. But I think that governments are now in a position to
do a better job of feeding the hungry. In Christian thought
there has always been food for the body—but there also must
be food for the soul. Food for the soul, Christian food, does
not come from the government.

What people and governments really need is a change
of attitude. There must be a change of consciousness to inspire them to be more strong, more independent, more the
individuals they were meant to be. Once in seminary I
wanted to give away money on Race Street, envisioning myself standing on a corner passing out ten-dollar bills to the
poor bums. But I soon realized that if I did that I would be
giving only a part of what was so desperately needed. True,
those men needed to survive physically, but they needed
more than that. What was lacking was an emphasis on bringing to these people some idea of Christ-consciousness, some
sense of the divine, some experience whereby they could
know that even those who helped them materially could
share with them the insight of the Holy Communion. And
that is the true idea of worship. Worship demands that God
be in the picture at all times. Strength is thus gained by a
group strength, and it is reinforced by one's private inner
world of devotion.

Faithful Christians know that worship is essential. The religious orders of the church have carried on this important work for centuries when others have neglected it. The work of a monastery or convent is to pray, to teach, to save. This is one of the reasons why, in the Episcopal church and others, liturgy, form, method, ways of worship have caused such debate and dissent. What, indeed, is the meaning of worship in our day?

Even though the public words of worship are important, even more important is the intention of worship. A sense of elevation must be a part of that experience. And because such a sense has been so lacking in our day, many feel that the mood, the reverence, the uplifting quality, and the mystery of worship have been debased. When the intention behind the words was confused, the quality of language was the first casualty. Words do convey thoughts. And when the words became inferior, the thoughts became inferior.

Suddenly people in the pews of all of the mainline denominations were involved in a fight for the right words to use in their worship liturgy. Was it going to be "You" or "Thou"? Was God going to be addressed as He, She, or It? Was it going to be a prayer book of "relevance" or a true reflection of the Gospel? Words that had been used for decades and centuries were declared to be obsolete, and a wrestling match began between clergy and laity. The clergymen in some churches would offer unison prayer, saying "You" at the same time the part of the congregation that didn't agree with him would loudly say "Thou." So it went, in many places, until it sounded like two radios going at once. Although all of the worshipers knew that God receives all prayer and worship, the great beauty and majesty of what can only be termed the Anglican style was rapidly fading. Louis Cassels wrote:

> To outsiders, the most conspicuous virtue of the Episcopal Church is the beauty of its liturgy . . . a strong voiced

Episcopal priest standing before an altar . . . you do not
know how poetic and uplifting corporate worship can be.
Episcopalians know.[1]

Whether they know at present is debatable. *Time* magazine, in its August 13, 1979 issue, devoted space to the "Battle of the Prayer Books." Several eminent literary critics were
quoted. The late W. H. Auden said of the new versions of the
Book of Common Prayer, "The Episcopal Church seems to
have gone stark raving mad." Cleanth Brooks of Yale called
it "pedestrian, second-rate, banal." William F. Buckley, Jr.,
said that the new book was "a Rolling Stone's Version." He
went on to say that the new Roman Catholic version of the
Mass "would offend the ears of Helen Keller."

In December 1979, at its Denver convention, the Episcopal church overwhelmingly voted themselves a new approach and a new direction in public worship. The delegates
adopted a "Conversation with God" prayer book for public
use. In it there were many alternatives for variety of expression; after all, the new book was a 1001-page volume.

After the convention made the action official, several
other writers published comments on liturgical language and
its heritage. The late venerable C. S. Lewis had already said
that "Liturgical prose needs to be not only very good but
very good in a very special way, if it is to stand up to reiter-
ated reading aloud." Of the new version (and its counter-
parts in the other denominations), columnist George Will
said: "Much of what is being done to religious language in
the name of 'relevance' is something a sensitive person cannot face, even once, without shuddering. God is not dead,
but he is powerfully embarrassed by books like *Are You
Running With Me, Jesus?* Somewhere in all this the wonder,
the awe, the majesty are left behind. God is not the guy
down the street. The power of words is not enhanced by the
'new approach.' "

The Gallup polls that indicated that the people in the

pews were not happy with the new Episcopal prayer book didn't seem to matter much. The fact that a columnist of the stature of James J. Kilpatrick was touched by the esthetic suicide committed by the Episcopal church meant very little in the battle of the prayer books. The depth of Kilpatrick's feeling is easily felt in his words: "Thomas Cranmer, the late Archbishop of Canterbury, was burned at the stake for heresy in 1556. At Denver next month his soul will go on writhing." Smith Hempstone, the Washington columnist, wrote that "to tinker with what G. K. Chesterton called 'the masterpiece of Protestantism' was a deed of monumental ecclesiastical folly and barefaced literary impertinence." In response to Hempstone, the head of the liturgical commission of the Episcopal church in New Jersey (and former national chairman of liturgy) wrote to me to say, "I object to this kind of journalism and I am surprised that you would be taken in by this kind of garbage."

When a church is in combat over worship, it is a partially crippled church. When it cannot agree on the very offering it should make to Almighty God, has stripped away much of the mystery of worship, has altered the Banquet of the Lord to three different versions (one of which could include coke and potato chips, or beer and pretzels), then it is surely "a church in frenzy." It is a church that desperately needs healing.

In the midst of this frenzy there are additional pleas for money, an economic crisis, and an effort to bind up the wounds. Official articles and letters are published that urge people to try to adjust to the new ways of public worship. There are those who predict that "within half a century or less, the 1979 version will probably be as revered as the 1928 Book of Common Prayer." I doubt it. I doubt it because, as John Scott said in *Christianity Today* (March 23, 1979), "Transcendence is now a secular quest—it constitutes a powerful challenge to the quality of our Christian public worship."

The clergy of all denominations have a way of going along with things. They are able to convince their people that the decisions that have been made are good ones and, therefore, that the laity should cooperate with them. To me, it is the Anglican way of muddling through. My friends in other denominations tell me that they call the same characteristic by other names in their traditions. An example from my personal knowledge comes to mind. A priest wrote to his congregation to remind them of all the former revisions of the prayer book and the trouble they had caused. He convinced them that each revision had been made "to help the people and to meet more fully the needs of the church."

To understand the confusion, an outsider (a non-Anglican, that is) need only know that there are now three possible kinds of service available on any given Sunday: If you prefer Rite I (the Holy Communion service using language similar to that of the former book), you come to the eight o'clock service. If you like Rite II (updated, lots of activity for all in the service), you come to the nine-thirty service. If you want a real free-style service, come at eleven. As Episcopalian Walter Cronkite would say: "And that's the way it is."

This kind of confusion is, of course, supposed to promote the peace and unity of the church. The result is that the church is so fragmented that never again will there be a standard of worship for all communicants.

Although I must again remind the reader that I am speaking primarily from my own background as a parish priest of the Episcopal church, I would not want him to forget that a great deal of what I am saying is true of each of the major American denominations today. Any reader, be he or she a pastor or a lay person, can easily make the transition to make my position clear in the light of another background.

So. It is not just a problem of language that has been so appalling in the Anglican tradition. It is the very thinking of Anglicanism itself that has been tampered with and disfigured. It is a face-lift gone wrong. A professional vestment maker told me, "I'm so damn sick of making weird vest-ments. I have refused to make chasubles and stoles out of burlap and plastic. First thing you know, some priest will want a stole out of sheet rubber!" The words "chasuble" and "stole" are familiar enough; it is the new thinking, and the content of meaning that is being put into such words, that betray the tradition.

The new "thinking" is the result of the decision that the church of today is medieval, inflicted with the errors of the past, and too patrician to be appealing. As the well-known editor of *The Living Church,* Carroll E. Simcox (now retired), put it, "The church was considered 'too otherworldly.' "

If anyone knows the inner workings of a church that has steadily advanced into frenzy, it is Simcox. Some time ago he wrote a little booklet called *Death By a Thousand Cuts.* In it he details the little nicks in the fabric of worship and thought, which eventually cause death, a slow and subtle death that is almost imperceptible to the one most con-cerned. It happens to a church, says Simcox, like the punish-ment meted out ages ago by the Japanese. "The condemned person was nicked, only slightly, in a thousand places on his body. None of the cuts by itself was fatal or even serious. But the result was the same. He bled to death. Slowly, but ever so surely."

Simcox sounds a note of warning for the great Anglican church when he says:

> Earlier in this century a great English Christian, G. K. Chesterton, viewed the decline of Christianity in his coun-try and ventured the view that Christianity had not been tried and found wanting, but rather that it had been found difficult and not been tried. I submit that what has some-times been called in the past "Prayer Book religion"—meaning Cranmerian Anglicanism—has not been tried and found wanting; it has been found difficult and demanding and has been tried only by some. In those who have "tried

it" seriously enough, God has created a high and holy and beautiful spirituality. But the promoters of the liturgical New Order seem willing to liquidate this treasure in the vain hope that in so doing they will make Anglicanism attractive to people who are shopping around for a cheap but pleasant version of the Christian religion. All that stands in their way is the old Prayer Book. If it is put to death by the thousand-cuts method—here a little nick, there a little nick—it will be so painless that nobody will notice it.

Until it is too late.[2]

Unfortunately, the person in the pew did not receive a revised prayer book but a new one. It contains a liturgy that for all intents and purposes was devised for the "now" generation, a reflection of the late 1960s and the 1970s. How futuristic that liturgical effort was is yet to be seen. It will be a long while before the results of a hope for larger attendance, greater stewardship, inner church unity, and dedication of youth will come forth from this kind of "renewal."

In the meantime, clergy will continue to lead services of worship. Some will lead their people in an atmosphere that unfolds the inner life. Others will devise unusual forms that always draw a crowd. Some will just carry on, muddling through. One priest told me, "I'm not going to do anything." So each clergyman will do "his thing," and each will be convinced of a different approach, all one in Christ but divided in form and structure. A complete parochialism pervades the church.

Some clergymen will confirm children at the age of five. Others will take the time-honored concept of insisting that children wait until they are ten or twelve and be confirmed by the bishop after instruction and evidence of understanding. One priest offers the perfect example of the confusion that now exists. He went away for a week. The substitute priest conducted the service, bringing with him various changes—including the administering of communion to a four-year-old; children of that age normally receive a blessing. When rector returned to the altar, passing by the four-year-old, the child started to scream and yell, "He didn't give me any! He didn't give me any!"

Some clergy will baptize infants; others will baptize only adults. Some will marry couples to their own strangely written vows; others will insist that the couple use only the set language of the church. Variety will be the spice of churches in all denominations. And as the church pleases everyone, so it will continue to displease itself.

The "holy secular" will be more and more in evidence because it has been courted by many clergy and has been given approval as a form of worship. Mixed values will comingle with mixed settings. And Christians will be left with no norms. The church has become worldly in the setting of heaven. The demand to take Christ down from the stained-glass windows to bring him closer to the people has been so overdone that Jesus may not be able to stand the crowd.

A scene that took place recently in Bradford Cathedral in England is quite representative of today's approach to worship and the thinking behind it. The service was to be a tribute to the life of motion picture star John Wayne. Three hundred people were in attendance. They arrived dressed as cowboys and Indians. Jesse James, General George Custer, members of a cowboy club, the legendary Cocksure McGrew, the notorious "Wild Bunch," one group right out of Fort Apache, and dozens of other characters from the Old West of America in Stetson hats—all were there in solemn tribute to John Wayne. In a Christian worship service.

They brought their guns. They stood silent for the procession of the Fifth Cavalry flag. They put their Colt 45's, their Winchester rifles, and their swords on the altar steps.

The Cathedral provost conducted the service. Dean Jackson praised John Wayne for his "two-fisted integrity."

He told the worshipers that cowboy ethics were like Christian ethics since "the Goody always wins." He said that their Western outfits were appropriate since the mayor and other city officials wore unusual outfits when they came to church. (The contrast between robes of authority and the casual dress of the American West seemed to please all present.)

The assembled congregation heard buglers sound the Last Post, and a three-gun cowboy salute was fired from the cathedral steps. The congregation rode off after the service into what was presumably a beautiful sunset.

So—the drawing card for attendance at worship these days can be a clever sermon title, a free gift, or the turning over of the pulpit to a ventriloquist's dummy. In Scarborough, England, the vicar of Saint Martin's Church had a dummy, Ambrose, deliver the sermon. A United Church of Christ minister in Merton, Wisconsin, Rev. Robert L. Anderson, suggests catchy sermon titles as bait for people. For example, if the preacher wants to sermonize on the Temptations in the Wilderness, his title might be "Jesus in the Back Country." If he is talking about the post-Resurrection appearances of Jesus, the sermon might be "A Beach Party with Jesus." Mr. Anderson offers other titles: "Wheeling and Dealing With Ezekiel," "After Christmas Clearance," "Laying It on the Laity," and finally one that may be prophetic— "Is the Church an Endangered Species?" The once-crowded Saint Bartholomew's Church in New York City advertised it all in the simple *New York Times* ad: "Contemporary Worship."

The *Philadelphia Inquirer* (November 29, 1979) reported that the vicar of Holy Trinity Church in London, Rev. Lawrence Hill, ran an advertisement in a theatre magazine offering the availability of his recently renovated church hall. The new tenant will be belly dancer Jill Chartell. Said Father Hill: "I thought an amateur play group might be grateful for the hall to hold rehearsals in. I never thought we would get a belly-dancing club here. However . . . I'm quite looking forward to it." A photograph of Father Hill and Miss Chartell accompanied the report. Miss Chartell was in costume.

One of the sentences that may be used at the beginning of the service of morning prayer in the Episcopal church is taken from Psalm 122: "I was glad when they said unto me, We will go into the house of the Lord."

For Evening Prayer, the sentence may be: "O worship the Lord in the beauty of holiness; let the whole earth stand in awe of him." (Psalm 96:9.)

Unless the major denominations can return to some outward and visual order in the years ahead, they may find that not many people will be glad to come into the house of the Lord. Nor will they any longer feel that they are worshiping in beauty and holiness. I am reminded of the words in the 1966 Beatles song entitled "Eleanor Rigby." "Father McKenzie, writing a sermon that no one will hear."

CHAPTER SIX

TENTS
TO TELEVISION

The dissension among clergy and laity created by the continuing controversy over worship and the forms of liturgy has been a major factor in the present frenzy in the church. But it may well be that such dissension is not so much the cause of the controversy as it is the result of a different aspect of that frenzy. As I noted earlier, we live in a day in which the meaning of words, indeed, the use of language itself, has shifted drastically. Theology speaks the language of the Christian faith and its tradition. Yet we are seeing today a major shift away from the ancient meanings of the words in Christian theology. We have seen that shift of meaning in the usage of the words in liturgy. Now it is time to examine the earthquake-producing faults in the underground levels of faith and tradition. Perhaps the people who are running around in such frenzy are doing so because an earthquake of major proportions has happened in the life of the church.

With the astonishing growth of the "fundamentalists" in all branches of Christendom, we are witnessing the power of words—spoken, written, and televised—to affect the basic meaning of Christianity in our day. I think that the speed and scope of the current shift in understanding the language of Christian faith is greater even than the one that occurred in Martin Luther's time. Whether that shift is a step forward or a step backward is a very debatable question. And it is the Fundamentalists who have forced the issue. With their cries of "Back to the Bible!" and "Back to the Original Faith!" they have forced the mainline denominations to raise the counterquestions: Yes, but which Bible? Yes, but which original faith?

So let us look again at the activities of the Fundamentalists—all the way from tents to television.

A Fundamentalist preacher is determined, committed, unbending, stern, and uncompromising. He believes his belief beyond belief. A perfect example is Rev. Daniel Aaron Rogers. His mother died on February 2, 1978. Mr. Rogers had her body frozen in a seated position. He bought a special jacket. He believed in the accounts of Jesus raising the dead. He believed so much that he tried to raise the dead himself. He believed that a special service of resurrection could bring his mother back to life. He tried twice and failed twice. (Even the funeral director had trouble going along with the second try.) Finally, the body was kept in a mortuary in Reeds Spring, Missouri. To that mortuary Pastor Rogers came with his wife to try to raise his mother again. At last they gave up and she was buried.

Pastor Rogers' comment was, "I guess the Lord needed Mother to be with my Father more than he wanted her to be with me."

It wasn't that she could not be raised, in his belief, but that God wanted her for another purpose. His basic belief was uncompromised. His very theology demanded it. What the Bible says is what the Bible commands. If the Bible says that Jesus raised the dead, then the Bible means that Christians can raise the dead. There is nothing ambiguous about that, in the mind of Pastor Rogers.

Another characteristic of the Fundamentalist churches

is that people can and do become crazed with the excitement of the presence of God. And a good preacher knows what he can do with that kind of excitement. When people come to a service in an atmosphere of expectancy, knowing that they can express themselves in physical ways, the preacher who urges them on has the power to bring them to the breaking point.

What could be more exciting than to be attending a debate between an evangelist like Bob Harrington and the atheist Madalyn Murray O'Hair? The two antagonists appear together on the platform prepared to go ten rounds in behalf of God and the Devil. Two thousand people packed the exhibition hall in Greenville, South Carolina.

Boos, cheers, screams—all for and against the champion of God and the champion of no god at all. The people there almost literally tore Madalyn O'Hair to bits, chanting "God! God! God!" When O'Hair said things like "Christians lead a stick-and-carrot life" and "Atheists don't need a Big Daddy in the Sky or a lollipop to be good," the audience went wild against her.

When Evangelist Harrington told the crowd that O'Hair was trying to get rid of "In God We Trust" on their coins, and that "she is pulling America apart brick by brick," they were ecstatic with joy. Then he gave them a real sentence, the kind that most followers of Harrington-type preachers love: "The day will come when this woman of the Devil will tremble in fear for her evil!"

Later on, the clever Madalyn commented on her brush with God. "Harrington has some charisma and a sense of humor, but he has nothing between the ears."

Among Fundamentalists, this event would be considered a major accomplishment, a crowd puller. Fundamentalists like crowds. Both the preachers and the faith healers like crowds. But sometimes things don't turn out so well when the crowd grows angry. In Rio de Janiero, Rev. David Martins de Miranda began a sermon on faith healing. But many of the two thousand present were not impressed. They tried to shout him down; they called him a fake. By the time it was over, twenty-one were dead, twenty-nine were injured. It was religion run amok.

Closer to home is the effect on the United States, indeed, on all the world, of the fanatic fundamentalist Ayatollah Khomeini in Iran. As I write these words, he still holds the fifty American hostages. The United States government tried to mobilize world opinion in favor of an economic boycott of Iran, hoping that this kind of pressure would free the hostages. Fearing the breakdown of the entire Mideast political and economic structure, both Israel and Egypt have suggested that they would be glad to have an American "military presence" stationed in their countries. And Russia has taken over Afghanistan. The United States has warned against a Russian incursion into Pakistan. Such is the power of a fanatic fundamentalist to trigger massive changes in the delicate interconnecting structure of modern civilization.

In the context of this discussion, it is most interesting to note that many leaders of the Middle Eastern countries, themselves Muslim, cry out that the Ayatollah is distorting, misusing, and totally degrading the traditional meaning of the Islamic faith. This while using the same religious words that are known to all Muslims.

To be sure, it is not possible to translate the Iranian religious situation directly in a one-to-one comparison with American Fundamentalists. Not yet.

But the history of extreme fundamentalism in America is instructive. Near me is the Bible Presbyterian Church under the famous Carl McIntire in Collingswood, New Jersey. Pastor McIntire has "condemned, criticized, opposed, accused, and upbraided" just about every conceivable social, political, and theological issue that exists (or can be made to exist). In the course of his endless crusades he has also accumulated enormous property holdings, including a major section of Cape May, New Jersey, where, according to newspaper reports, he owed thousands of dollars in back taxes. And he goes on, in old age, receiving the bequests of wealthy ladies who believe in his brand of Bible elixir.

A different, more theological, aspect of American Fundamentalism is the concept of the Second Coming of Christ. Probably no other doctrine is more dear to the Fundamentalist heart as the Second Coming. Actually, it is a difficult and puzzling concept to most theologians. But not if it is taken literally. In North Hollywood, the First Assembly of God Church pastor, D. Leroy Sanders, thinks that the Second Coming will occur in this generation. He is making plans to help those who will be left behind (if they are) when the great event takes place, that is, "when we shall be caught up together with them in the clouds to meet the Lord . . ." Pastor Sanders and his official board amended the bylaws of the church so that others could take over the necessary administrative duties when they themselves were "caught up." Mr. Sanders has also suggested that if entire families think that they might go, they can change their wills and leave the money to the church.

In America, anyone can be a preacher. The mere fact that extensive study and training might be required isn't questioned very much once the honorific title "Reverend" is placed before the name. Mail-order religion can grant anyone a bogus ordination and even a theological degree. And such is the mission of such groups as the Universal Life Church. Its founder, Kirby J. Hensley, has awarded more than 6.5 million ordinations and more than 30,000 charters for churches. Not including doctor of divinity degrees and doctor of philosophy degrees at $100 per degree. For five dollars, anyone can have himself, herself, or a friend—elevated at once to sainthood. The income to the Universal Church from all this is said to be in excess of $1 million a year.

The list of Fundamentalist evangelists who have trod the sawdust trail from tent to radio to television is long and growing longer. In 1973, St. Martin's Press published a book called *The Preachers,* by James Morris. In that book, the author gives a detailed account of the life and works of such preachers as A. A. Allen, Oral Roberts, C. W. Burpo, Rev. Ike, Carl McIntire, Kathryn Kuhlmann, Billy James Hargis, the Armstrongs (father and son), and Billy Graham. Of them all, Billy Graham has retained the respect and esteem of countless thousands who applaud his honest efforts for Christ.

Others have not fared so well. A. A. Allen died in a hotel room with a vial of pills by his side and $2,309.00 in his wallet—while a tape recording of his voice denied rumors of his death. His life, and all the scandal attached to it—including fraud and liquor—would make a movie of monumental proportions.

The indiscretions of Billy James Hargis and his activities at Tulsa College (which he blamed on "genes and chromosomes") ruined his career. Hargis was a remarkable speaker who could drive his audiences mad with excitement. When he slammed his fist down on the pulpit and then punctuated every sentence with another slam, people listened.

Rev. Ike makes one think of that famous statement that A. A. Allen made to the fake evangelist, Marjoe, "Son, let me tell you something. Do you know how to tell when a revival meeting is over? Do you know when God's saying to move on to the next town? I'll tell you: When you can turn people on their heads and shake them and no money falls out. Then you know God's saying to you, 'Move on, son!' "

I have met and interviewed Kathryn Kuhlmann, who continued to be a mystery to me as long as she lived. She was indeed an unusual woman. Her healings were often questioned and denounced in books such as *Healing: A Doctor in Search of a Miracle,* by William A. Nolen, M.D. However, many thousands of people believe that she was God's agent in healing them. To say that she appealed to and was able to heal only those who themselves were Fundamentalists is per-

haps accurate, but may be misleading. In any
never doubted that God was at work through her
⎯⎯Oral Roberts has moved into a different category among
the Fundamentalist preachers and healers since his tent healing days. With his college, his television church, and his new
hospital (if he manages to find his way through the maze of
litigation that it has brought about), he has reached the ranks
of the "superstar" evangelists. Roberts is the subject of "An
Insider's Report" in the book *Give Me That Prime-Time Religion* by Jerry Sholes, published by Hawthorn Books, 1979.
Unfortunately, one month after the publication of this incredible array of incisive allegations, Sholes was brutally,
viciously beaten—but not robbed—in a Tulsa, Oklahoma,
parking lot. He required plastic surgery to repair his face and
right cheekbone.

It is useful to review the characteristic marks of Fundamentalism as they are manifested in the rules and regulations
of Oral Roberts University. The marks of maturity, as out-
lined in the 259–page Oral Roberts University catalog, include
the wearing of a shirt and tie every weekday for men, *no*
wearing of short skirts by women, no "excessive" public dis-
plays of emotion, no profanity, no smoking, no gambling, no
cheating, no drinking, no immorality, no drugs. And a clean
and orderly room. Students must be prompt to class, must
attend chapel, and must not loiter in darkened areas of the
campus. Moreover, students are to remind others of their
faults if they violate the honor code—and they must sign that
honor code in order to complete registration. The signing
ceremony is held in the chapel.

It is also the university community's view that one
should not feel restricted by the code. Such a negative attitude to the code is thought to be abnormal. Bible-fundamen-
talists follow the rules. Many educational psychologists
would say that these students are trained to be behaviorist-
perfectionists.

The most complex family-run church was the Worldwide Church of God. Herbert W. Armstrong and his son, Garner Ted Armstrong, amassed a fortune with their radio and television religious programs, which espoused both secular and religious truths. Who can forget Garner Ted and his program "The World Tomorrow?"

Impressive in his handsomeness, and with an actor's voice, Garner Ted Armstrong charmed his listeners, leading them down the road to Doomsday, pharisaical behavior, and good works. Actually, the church is or was a cult. *(Is* or *was* depends on the survival of the church through a barrage of scandal, both personal and financial.) When Herbert Armstrong excommunicated Garner Ted because of his questionable personal life, the church's financial condition began to deteriorate alarmingly. The once-impressive campus in Tyler, Texas, was sold for a sum well below its $10 million valuation.

Garner Ted now has his own church—"The Church of God International." This organization is run by a staff of 177 people who, in 1975, mailed out more than 61 million pieces of literature.

In 1978, Garner Ted was the subject of an article in *Hustler* magazine entitled "In Bed With Garner Ted—America's Promiscuous Preacher." It was a fascinating and titillating exposé of Mr. Armstrong's sex life. Shortly after the *Hustler* article appeared, a group of disenchanted former workers in the Church of God International produced a slick-paper publication closely resembling the church's Ambassador College magazine *The Ambassador Report*. In it the authors attempted to show that Garner Ted had surpassed the image of that fabled lecher Elmer Gantry.

The amount of money involved in a religious "empire" such as the Worldwide Church of God is staggering. When a Fundamentalist can be convinced that a cause is "biblical," his commitment can be so great that he will give immense amounts of money to it. One man who lost a fortune was the chess champion, Bobby Fischer. He is reported to have sent the Armstrongs $61,200—and the devotion of fifteen years of his life.

When pastors of the mainline town and country churches present their denominational stewardship programs and plead for their parishioners to take home offering envelopes, they are asking for peanuts compared to the money-raising efforts of the radio and television Fundamentalists. And while the mainline churches are in frenzy over attendance and finances, the Fundamentalist preachers and churches are flooded with mail-order money.

When the Fundamentalist preachers fail, they fail in strange and bizarre ways. One pastor was arrested for voluntary manslaughter in Las Vegas. He had strangled his wife because he believed that she was possessed by demons. He said that she growled like an animal, foamed at the mouth, and uttered strange cries. With extreme care he burned the paper towels she had used to wipe her face. And a serpent appeared in the flames. When the pastor tried to exorcise his wife, he and the others with him all began screaming and foaming. Then the pastor's wife "slithered around like a snake." The pastor wrapped his belt around her neck. She "went limp." The pastor thought that he had healed her so he put her to bed. She was dead.

However, the Pentecostal fundamentalists are not the only ones whose religious practices result in bizarre episodes. An English vicar and a Methodist minister tried an exorcism in an Anglican church in Gawber, England. The ceremony lasted all night in Saint Thomas Church. When the subject returned home, he immediately killed his wife.

So extreme can this kind of approach to religion become that misguided clergy, who do not take into account their need for additional psychiatric and psychological training, can and do inflict grievous harm on already sick people. That is, some clergy are as sick as those they are trying to help. An incident in West Germany demonstrates what can happen in such cases. Two priests and a lay couple treated a Würzburg

University theology student for nine months. They claimed that she had no fewer than six demons inhabiting her mind and body, including Adolf Hitler, the Emperor Nero, and Judas Iscariot. Medical doctors had failed to cure her of epilepsy. Following that unsuccessful treatment, she fell back on her strong Fundamentalist upbringing. She concluded that she was demon-possessed. And when the exorcism rites of the priests and her parents drove her completely insane, the local legal authorities brought the exorcists into court and found them guilty.

When I was scheduled to give a talk on ESP in an Episcopal parish in southern New Jersey, the newspaper notice triggered a quick response from the Assembly of God church. They objected to the announced meeting because they said it was "evil." Someone had read, or heard of, my book *The Spiritual Frontier* and learned of my interest in the paranormal aspects of the human mind and spirit. The knee-jerk response was a flood of phone calls, including one that warned me to stay out of town. Another caller was sure that I was "in league with Satan."

As I indicated earlier, the Fundamentalist mentality is not at all confined to the "storefront" churches but, in fact, is more and more often found in churches of the mainline denominations. A Presbyterian pastor in Wingo, Kentucky, told his congregation, in all seriousness, that he was "the spirit of Elijah." He now plans to convert all the nations of the world, all the while warning his people against false prophets. His fellow clergy refuse to comment except to say that "he is sincere."

Once a clergyman gets steamed up about something he often uses his position to speak out on it. And the reason why the church is in frenzy is precisely because so many clergy have spoken out on the wrong things. With all the zeal at their command they spread the word about whatever "cause" is uppermost in their minds. And, in our society, the more charisma an individual clergyman has the more easily he can attract followers.

For example, Rev. Paul Tinlin, pastor of the Evangel Assembly of God Church in Hoffman Estates, Illinois, thinks that we should televise the execution of criminals on the national networks. This is the same line of reasoning followed by the Ayatollah Khomeini in televising the public whipping of men who had been convicted of frequenting prostitutes. It is indicative of the way that the Fundamentalist preachers are reaching out to a wider audience than their local churches provide. It leads directly to the use of the mass-market television "religious" programs that we are now coming to know as "the electronic church."

Mainline churches, depending as they do on the eleven o'clock Sunday morning worship service with personal attendance expected, find that the new appeal of religious broadcasting is a growing threat to their continued existence. If regular parishioners are annoyed by the deluge of "renewal" programs devised by national and regional leaders, or even their own local clergy, then there is a ready means of escape. Such people can still "go to church" by tuning in their television sets. To be sure, the "TV pastors" are well aware of this situation. So they now go after prime-time schedules that will reach not only the people who are unhappy with their own churches but also those who still attend the services at eleven o'clock on Sunday morning. And so the television preachers get attention from both groups. From their point of view, they can easily convince people that "if Jesus were living today, he would not be preaching a Sermon on the Mount, he would be preaching a Sermon on TV."

 It is instructive to review the statistics that demonstrate the influence of the electronic church. And even more instructive to remember that whatever set of numbers is used to describe the phenomenon, those numbers are out of date almost as rapidly as they can be assembled. Two years ago,

The New York Times published an article by Kenneth Briggs on this subject. At the time, there were more than one thousand Christian radio stations, twenty-five Christian-controlled television outlets, and almost countless individual religious radio and television programs. A group of these religious broadcasters have now banded together in a National Christian Television Network. These network stations claim that they reach more than 114 million radio listeners and more than 14 million television viewers each week.

It is not just idle futuristic speculation to say that the day is coming when a television receiver will be able to project a three-dimensional religious program into our living rooms. This will provide an almost real experience of being in church. It is this kind of "mass media" church that the religious broadcasters envision as the best possible means of spreading the Word of God throughout the world.

This kind of threat to our current and conventional worship services was brought home to me in a very vivid way recently when a parishioner of mine told me that when she watched a certain TV preacher and he offered communion to his viewers, she went into the kitchen, poured a glass of wine, and had Communion with him. She also sent her newly discovered spiritual leader a great amount of money. For this "gift" she received a small vial of "healing oil" that she kept on the lamp table. When told to do so by the TV preacher, she dabbed a drop or so of oil on her forehead during each program. This healed her of whatever ailments she had at the moment.

What effect is the new electronic church having on those who listen and view in their own homes? Is it effecting a change of consciousness on the part of religious people today? Will it help to change society for the better? More specifically, will it, indeed, bring the Word of God into every home? Will it ever replace the discipline of worship with others in fellowship and communion in a hallowed place?

Such questions are difficult to answer because of the

speed with which the electronic media are changing. For example, the new system whereby the viewer at home can respond directly to the television announcer (or preacher!) by pushing buttons on his set is only the first step in a soon-to-come two-way visual communication link between viewer and broadcaster. (An elementary version of such a system is already being used in Columbus, Ohio.) Among other things, this surely means that the objection to the electronic church as a church in isolation (like a drive-in church) is no longer valid. And if, using the three-dimensional system of transmission, the preacher and the choir are seen to "appear" in one's living room, will not the viewer feel the full impact of the television preacher's personal charisma in an even more forceful way than he does today? But I wonder how the viewer will feel when, at the end of the service, he reaches out to shake the preacher's hand—and discovers that it is nothing but thin air.

My own feeling is that in this kind of electronic wizardry we will not have worship but entertainment. Most likely, such televised programs will offer the same kind of syrupy interviews with famous folk, a great many "Gospel song stylists," and a star in the form of the program's host (the preacher-evangelist), all wrapped up in the selling of a sweet and easy road to God, our kind old Grandfather-in-the-Sky whom we address as casually as we do the friend down the block and whose main business is to forgive us all our minor peccadilloes, to protect motherhood and our way of life, and—if we faithfully send in our love offerings to the television station (whose call letters, phone number, and post-office box number are conveniently shown at the bottom of the screen)—will make us healthy, wealthy, and wise.

Such is already the approach of the nationally televised "700 Club" and the "P.T.L. Club." Throughout these programs one finds tears, personal traumas, and piteous fears that our great leader may not be able to stay on the air unless we send in more money. We are offered elegant editions of the Bible if only we love God and support the TV ministry. And so we are caught up in an "industry" that far surpasses the average annual budget of any of the major Protestant denominations.

Dr. Robert Schuler will easily pay for his $18-million glass Crystal Cathedral. On the Sunday appointed for a special offering, men wearing hard hats and using wheelbarrows took up the collection. It amounted to $1,251,376 in cash and checks contributed by some five thousand persons attending the three services. Oral Roberts plans to build a $250-million City of Faith medical complex, which will include a thirty-story hospital. God told him that it was to be opened debt-free. And he will do it.

A new and very serious aspect of the electronic church is reported at some length in the September 24, 1979, issue of *U.S. News and World Report.* The front cover of this issue has a photograph of one of the television preachers. Superimposed on the picture is the title: "Preachers in Politics."

The subheading of the article itself is this sentence: "Conservative ministers and lobbyists are out to arouse the 'sleeping giant' of American politics—millions of evangelical Christians who say they have enough votes to change the course of U.S. history in the 1980's." The text of the article goes on to show that the television preachers have formed a loose alliance that is designed to influence both elections and laws at every level of the American political system—all the way up to the White House. It is said that there are 50 million "born again" Christians (mostly Protestant) and an additional 30 million "morally conservative" Roman Catholics. There are a few million Mormons and Orthodox Jews who might be expected to vote with such a bloc.

Television evangelist M. G. "Pat" Robertson has said that, counting Protestants and Catholics together, "We have enough votes to run the country. And when the people say, 'We've had enough,' we are going to take over."

This threat (or promise!) is buttressed by some recent political victories. Religious groups helped defeat such liberals as Democratic Senators Dick Clark of Iowa and Thomas McIntyre of New Hampshire. Other such groups blocked the ERA in states from Nevada to Virginia, defeated ordinances on the rights of homosexuals, and passed laws protecting church-related schools.

The prime mover in this effort is a group that calls itself The Christian Voice, with headquarters in Pasadena, California. Membership in the group is expected to reach one million by the November 1980 elections. It is said that sixteen members of Congress are on the advisory committee and that the organization will spend $3 million on the 1980 political campaign. Members of Congress will be rated on a "morality scale" according to their stand on issues like homosexuality, pornography, government spending, and defense. These "ratings" will then be sent to five thousand ministers, with the suggestion that they encourage voters to vote against forty incumbents blackballed by The Christian Voice. "The beauty of it is that we don't have to organize these voters," said a Christian Voice lobbyist. "They already have their own television networks, publications, schools, meeting places, and respected leaders who are sympathetic to our goals."

The amount of money that is controlled by the TV pastors is awesome, as I have mentioned above. It is said that the top three preachers (Robertson, Falwell, and Bakker) collect a combined total annually of $150 million. *Each of their operations grosses about twice as much money as the Republican and Democratic candidates spent on the last presidential campaign.* The "Campus Crusade for Christ," led by Rev. Bill Bright, has set a goal of $1 *billion* for a worldwide campaign in the media. The first $100 million of this has already been raised.

The *U.S. News and World Report* article goes on to state that "while conservative Christians become more militant, the vote-swaying power of liberal churches is generally regarded as declining from its peak in the anti-war and civil-rights campaigns of the 1960's. Another problem for the liberal groups is their leftward drift into Third World causes, led by the National Council of Churches."

In terms of the political effect of conservative Christians on American Life, Professor Jeffrey K. Hadden, president of the Association for the Sociology of Religion, has said, "So many zealous people are getting up in arms that the 1980's could bring the biggest religious clash in politics since the struggle over civil rights."

Any discussion of the effects of fundamentalist religion on the life of the church today would be inadequate if it failed to deal with the wide appeal of the religious cults in the United States. The frenzy in the church, especially in its "tents to television" aspects, is surely caused by the strong appeal of the religious cults to many thousands of members of the mainstream churches. No responsible church leader can view the cults and their followers as being in any way a part of the mainstream of the Christian Church. And yet the cults are increasing in number and variety every day. The church must be concerned with them because a great many church members are turning to them in a search for what seems to be lacking in the mainline denominations.

What is a cult? One definition goes like this: "A cult is a religious perversion. It is a belief and practice in the world of religion which calls for devotion to a religious view or leader centered in false doctrine. It is an organized heresy." Another definition made by a well-known scholar is this: "By the term 'cult,' I mean nothing derogatory to any group so classified. A cult, as I define it, is any religious group which differs significantly in some one or more respects as to belief or practice from those religious groups which are regarded as the normative expressions of religion in our total culture." Walter Martin refines that definition a bit by adding: "A cult might also be defined as a group of people gathered about a specific person or persons' interpretation of the Bible."

It seems to me that today there are cults and practices that have deviated so very far from *any* kind of religious norm, whether Christian or not, that they represent a totally new and different stream of faith for their followers. The fact that some of these are to be found within many Christian congregations makes the situation even more difficult to comprehend. And since some of them continue to use Christian vocabulary and Christian liturgical forms, however grotesque may be the meaning that they have put into those words and forms, church leaders and lay people are finding it almost impossible to deal with them. Let me give a few examples.

At this writing, the most attention is being given to the Church of Scientology. This group, founded in 1954 by a former science-fiction writer named L. Ron Hubbard, now has at least 3 million followers. Its annual revenues amount to hundreds of millions of dollars, most of which are tax-exempt. In October 1979, a federal judge held nine members of the church guilty of conspiracy or of stealing government documents about the church. The statement made by the U. S. attorney includes this paragraph:

> On behalf of the Church of Scientology, top officials directed and engaged in a massive and highly disciplined conspiracy to burglarize offices of the United States government, to steal confidential documents, and to obstruct justice by committing perjury before a federal grand jury.

The federal prosecutor went on to show that the church operated like a well-run spy agency, infiltrating government offices and picking file cabinets bare at the Internal Revenue Service in a search for documents on the Scientologists' tax-exempt status. The documents showed that the church operatives were employed by the IRS and the Justice Department. More than fifteen thousand such documents were taken. Other documents were released which indicated that the Scientologists had infiltrated the American Medical Association and the National Institute of Mental Health as part of an effort to discredit these organizations. Both groups have been critical of the mental-therapy techniques advocated by Ron Hubbard in his book *Dianetics: The Modern Science of Mental Health*, which is the basic textbook and bible of the Church of Scientology.

What is the appeal of Scientology? Perhaps the best way to see this is to read some of the comments made by well-known people who belong to the group.

"It's nice to know you can be a cause of your life as well as an effect," says John Travolta, twenty-three, of his training in Scientology. "It's a logical and very sane way of living. I don't get upset as easily as I used to. I don't think I could have handled my success as well without it."

Speaking of a low point in her career some years ago, Karen Black has said, "It [Scientology] made me real happy. Mr. Hubbard has a very formidable technology for the relief of the despair that people carry around with them. It makes you very free."

Actress Judy Norton-Taylor, twenty, who plays Mary Ellen on "The Waltons," became a member of the cult at age thirteen. She is now an "auditor" (counselor) herself. "It's been very helpful to me in my work," she has said. "It's made me more secure and given me more confidence in myself."

NBC Sportscaster and former San Francisco 49'ers quarterback John Brodie believes that Scientology provided the cure for an injured arm in 1970 after unsuccessful regular medical treatment: "It wasn't a miracle or anything, it's so simple and so logical and so workable."

Jazz bass player Stanley Clarke, twenty-eight, became a member a few years ago. "It's totally changed my life," he says. "I've got a lot more understanding about myself, about others. I don't do drugs anymore. All I can say is the Scientologists really know what's happening."

It is clear that the primary emphasis in all of these statements (and countless others like them) is on the individual rather than the group. Within the cult, the individual is searching for identity, for self-understanding and some kind of relationship with other people. But the "relationship" is almost always one-sided; that is, the individual is concerned with his or her relationship to other people, not with theirs to him. A secondary emphasis is on an interpretation of the present and the future which will provide a dominating theme for the individual's life, peace of mind, and/or harmony with reality. The notion of a transcendent God may or may not be necessary in this scheme of things.

In other cults the idea of God is quite necessary. Rev. Sun Myung Moon is believed to be God by his followers. When he founded his religious movement in the early 1950s in Korea, he called himself "Moon-Jesus." His Unification Church has attracted followers who find that the "apathy" and "hypocrisy" of the mainline churches, as they see it, has turned them off. In Moon's church they believe that they have found vision, zeal, love, and discipline. They believe that Christ failed to gain complete salvation and that a Korean-born messiah, probably Moon himself, will fulfill the task. Moon is quoted in a *Time* magazine article as saying: "I will conquer and subjugate the world. I am your brain." And, as the second Christ, his followers ask no questions of him, sell flowers and candy, and are now moving into wholesale and retail operations that bring in millions of dollars. Moon's book *The Divine Principle* is a mixture of Christian vocabulary, occultism, and dualism, and is the "Bible" for his followers.

Anyone who reads current newspapers and magazines has learned that the Unification Church is now almost continually in court. Hundreds of parents have been greatly concerned about what this cult is doing to the minds of their

children who have been converted to it. They are filing lawsuits and are forming associations of anti-Moon groups.
Much notice has been given to the "deprogramming" activities of Ted Patrick and others who conduct counter-brain-
washing programs, first resorting to abduction to rescue the
young converts from the various Moon communities. Although Moon spokesmen acknowledge that more than four
hundred "Moonies" have gone through deprogramming,
they insist that more than half of these have subsequently
returned to the Unification Church.

One of the unanswered questions about the followers of
Moon is why young men and women from well-to-do families join the cult. One reason seems to be that these young
people have had little or no firm attachment to the mainline
denominations, yet are striving for some sense of stability in
an uncertain world, for some sense of morality in a world
that seems to have none.

Anyone who looks at the cults today cannot fail to be
concerned about the People's Temple and Rev. Jim Jones.
Many people are saying about the suicides in Guyana, "If
this is religion, then I want no part of it!"

In a major feature article in *The New York Times Magazine* (January 7, 1979), Professor Robert Jay Lifton of Yale
University wrote that the death drama at Jamestown "jolts us
not only because of its incredible statistics and the dreadful
power of a mad leader over his followers, but because we
sense in it a terrible caricature of real struggles taking place
in American society."

Dr. Lifton goes on to say that there are three basic issues
involved in any effort to understand what happened: (1) the
pattern of killing and dying that took place; (2) the quality of
obedience behind the pattern; (3) the psychological and historical readiness of people for such a cult experience.

To be sure, the first of these three issues is rarely apparent when we are discussing the run-of-the-mill cults on the
American religious scene. But Dr. Lifton surely speaks of all

or most cults in implying that the second and third of the issues may always be capable of exploding into "killing and dying." And the people who take the first step down that road never seem to be aware of where the road may lead.

We cannot close this review of the cults without looking briefly at the strange and continuing fascination that young people have found in the religions of the East. During the 1970s, millions of Americans were caught up in what has since been called a "neo-Oriental religious revival." Most of these Americans were young people in their twenties, and a great many of them were drawn to these Eastern religious groups from the mainline Protestant churches. True, many of them were only on the periphery of the churches; even so, their parents were solid, churchgoing people. What happened?

In the basement of an Episcopal church in Cambridge, Massachusetts, Sufi dancers meet twice a week, chanting the Koran and whirling like dervishes in a ritual that has nothing to do with Episcopalian tradition. The dancers are not Sufi Persians. They are young Americans.

Within walking distance of Harvard Square, in Cambridge, and of the main gate at the entrance to the Berkeley campus of the University of California, dozens of groups of devotees of Eastern religions meet to practice their various forms of meditation and devotion. One can find such groups on or near the campus of any college in America today.

Professor Harvey Cox, chairman of the Department of Applied Theology at Harvard, and himself a Baptist, spent three years investigating these groups. His questions were: What has provoked this neo-Oriental religious movement? Who are the people caught up in it? Why have they left the more conventional religious life (or none at all) to become adherents of these religious groups? What does all this mean for American culture and the American church?

Dr. Cox said: "During the first several weeks of the study, my students and I had a marvelous time. Together

and separately, we attended dozens of lectures, inquirers'
meetings, worship services, and study circles . . . but as a
Christian and a professional theologian, I realized that I was
neither a genuine Oriental pilgrim nor an authentic seeker.
So I became a participant not because I thought there was
actually something in it for me, but because I wanted to
nourish my capacity for empathy . . . to find out what I could
about the lure of the East on the visceral level."

Curiously enough, Dr. Cox discovered, much to his own
surprise, that nearly all the people he met had personal reasons for their interest in these groups that had little or nothing to do with the official teachings of the groups' leaders.
This then led him to begin to look for what it really was that
the individuals found when they joined up. In the course of
this part of the investigation, Dr. Cox discovered that participants tend to be in their late teens or early twenties. "The
twenties are the prime time for 'turning East,' " he says.

These religious groups are made up almost exclusively
of white, middle- and upper-middle-class young people.
They are from all religious denominations, with a few more
from the liberal Protestant communions (Episcopal, Presbyterian, Congregational, and Unitarian) than the membership
percentages might suggest. Most of them have been in college although, of course, many of them are college dropouts.
There is a fairly even balance between men and women,
although the leadership of the groups seems to be male-dom-
inated. More members of the movements come from urban
areas than from rural towns and villages. But it is the urban,
middle-class, educated population from which the liberal
denominations draw most of their members. Few of the
"seekers" come from strongly atheistic or from unusually pi-
ous homes. Writes Cox: "They seem to have received some
religion from their parents, but not enough to satisfy them."

Because Dr. Cox's conclusions have so much to say to
the whole frenzy in the church today, they are very much
worth noting here.

First, most of the members of these movements seem to be looking for simple human *friendship*. The stories they told were of loneliness, isolation, and the search for a supportive community. Cox paraphrases a great many replies to his queries:

> They seem to care for me here. I was bummed out, confused, just wandering around. When I first came here I didn't know what they were talking about. They all seemed crazy, and I told them so. But that didn't seem to bother them. They took me in. They made me feel at home. Now I feel like I'm a part of it, and an important part, too. I belong here. It's where I was meant to be.

Second, many of the young people who turn to the Eastern religions seem to be looking for a way to experience life directly, without the intervention of rational ideas and concepts. They are looking for a firsthand experience, not through textbooks or through some preacher's sermons. What they say, according to Dr. Cox, is:

> All I got at any church I ever went to were sermons or homilies *about* God, *about* "the peace that passes understanding." Words, words, words. It was all up in the head. I never really *felt* it. It was all abstract, all up in the head, never direct, always somebody else's account of it. It was dull and boring. I'd sit or kneel or stand. I'd listen to or read prayers. But it seemed lifeless. It was like reading the label instead of eating the contents.
> But here it really happened to me. I experienced it myself. I don't have to take someone else's word for it.

Dr. Cox goes on to say that this feeling for direct experience became more understandable when he noticed that nearly all of these Eastern religions include instruction in some form of spiritual discipline. "Initiates learn the primary techniques of prayer, chanting, contemplation, or meditation. Teachers rely not only on words, as in most Western religious training, but also on actual techniques—either quite simple, as in transcendental meditation, or complex, as in Zen—for inducing the desired forms of consciousness."

Third, some of these young people are looking for authority when they turn to the Eastern movements. They earnestly want some kind of truth, some message, that they can trust completely. "They join these groups as refugees from uncertainty and doubt." Here is Cox's paraphrase of the message he got from a number of the young people:

> I tried everything. I read all the books, went to lectures, listened to different teachers. But all that happened was that I got more confused. I couldn't think straight any more. I couldn't get myself together or make any decisions. Then I met him [the Guru], and what he said finally made sense. Everything finally clicked. I knew he was for real. I could tell just from the way he spoke that he knew. Now my confusion is over.

Professor Cox himself concludes that the quest for authority results from a wide range of factors: the dissolution of conventional moral codes; the erosion of traditional authorities; the recent emergence of what Alvin Toffler calls "overchoice." As a consequence, a great many people, young and old, are suffering from a kind of "choice-fatigue." They ache for some kind of authority that will simplify, straighten out, assure—anything or anyone who can make their choices fewer and less complicated. For thousands, that search ends with some Eastern guru (even though he may have been born in Brooklyn).

Finally, a few people told Dr. Cox and his investigators that they had deliberately turned their backs on what they considered "the effete, corrupt, or out-worn religious tradition of the West." They said that they were looking for something more *natural.* That is, they thought that they had found a religion that was still unspoiled, simple, and fresh. But, in fact, it seemed easier for them to talk about what they had turned *from* than why they had turned *toward* the East. They were saying something like this:

> Western civilization is shot. It is nothing but technology and power and rationalization, corrupted to its core by power and money. It has no contact with nature, feeling, spontaneity. What we need to do now is learn from the Oriental peoples who have never been ruined by machines and science, who have kept close to their ancestors' simplicity. Western religion has invalidated itself. Now only the East is possible.

Cox makes the interesting comment that these were the people who were often the best educated and most widely read of all those who were turning to the East: "They could often cite evidence more specifically and phrase their arguments more clearly than the others . . . to me their decision to turn East often seemed to have some of the quality of a purification ritual . . . they seemed to be trying to shed the tainted and the impure."

Professor Cox provides a summary and an evaluation of his research in terms that are extremely important to anyone who would understand what I am calling "the frenzy in the church" today. His remarks are worth quoting at some length here:

> Curiously, it is precisely America's receptivity, its eagerness to hear, explore, and experience, that creates the most difficult barrier to our actually learning from Eastern spirituality. The very insatiable hunger for novelty, for intimacy, even for a kind of spirituality that motivates so many Americans to turn toward the East also virtually guarantees that the turn will ultimately fail.
>
> The final paradox is that Easterners have never claimed to be able to save the West. Frequently they deny

having any interest in doing so, even if they could. They rarely send missionaries here, and they accept Western novices with reluctance. Although Westernized versions of Eastern faiths often claim to bring salvation to the West, at this point they betray the spirit of their sources, and actually worsen the Western dilemma by advertising more than they can deliver.

The spiritual crisis of the West will not be resolved by spiritual importations or individual salvation. It is the crisis of a whole civilization, and one of its major symptoms is the belief that the answer must come from Elsewhere. The crisis can be met only when the West sets aside myths of the Orient, and returns to its own primal roots.[1]

The point that I want to make in the strongest of terms is this: In all of these cults, movements, and neo-religions, no matter what their mode of presentation, whether ancient or modern, there is not the kind of prayer and quiet meditation that is based on a crucified and risen Christ. There is not the kind of corporate worship that the ancient Christian tradition has given us. There is not the living hope that is the gift of God to our world.

It seems to me that it is just the lack of these ancient truths that has caused the frenzy in the church.

CHAPTER SEVEN

FUTURE CHURCH

What was once the headquarters of the Episcopal Diocese of Pennsylvania is now a disco. It is called "The Second Story" and is a private club catering to a "Studio 54" type of crowd. The abandoned chapel is the centerpiece of the club. There are stained glass windows portraying Mary, which now hang behind the bar. The customary church fixtures are used throughout the place as an accent to the decor. The baptismal font now holds popcorn.

Could this be the fate of many churches in the future? Maybe it could.

In 1969, ten years ago at this writing, Dr. Roland W. Tapp was associate editor of religious books for The Westminster Press, the official publishing house of the United Presbyterian Church. He was asked to conduct a full-scale research project designed to look ahead down the road that the Protestant churches were going. In his subsequent report, he listed twenty-five trends that he could identify and the changes that they implied in the life of the churches by the year A.D. 2000.

If Dr. Tapp made these predictions today, we would

have to wait and see how accurate they were. The fact that they were made ten years ago and that many of them are obviously true makes his insights worth taking seriously. Now retired and living in Florida, he recently told me: "I have seen very little since 1969 to convince me that I was completely off my rocker in suggesting that these are definite possibilities for the church in the year 2000."

Let us consider those predictions, now nearly eleven years old. The summary statements appeared in the house organ of the Protestant Church-owned Publishers Association, and were later reproduced in the June 16, 1969, issue of *Publishers Weekly,* the trade journal of the publishing industry:

1. The church is going to have to go through the fundamentalist-liberal fight of 50 years ago all over again, with sharper polarization.

The organized church has not seen the last of this, and it will probably continue to escalate. Dr. Tapp sees this kind of polarization as more subtle and more sophisticated, but less theological. One of the dilemmas of the fundamentalist is that he often believes that Fundamentalism is theological. This happens because of biblical language and the absolute manner in which it is used without question. Such use of the biblical vocabulary is ordinarily seen in the stories of people's behavior patterns. These are taken to "prove" that the Lord is at work and that the Bible is true. Dr. Tapp sees this as psychological in origin and as a pattern that will lead to more and more religious conflict unless it can be transposed into some positive use within the community of faith. Unless it can be successfully managed it will split the church, since it divides those who are accustomed to an accepted norm of religious approach from those who embrace the "force-feed" effect of the Gospel. Perhaps the most important thing to note at this point is that we may be dealing, not with a radical fundamentalism but a kind of subtle and powerful embracing of an easy approach to Jesus.

2. There will be a growing trend towards merger with Roman Catholics at practical levels. But the cooperation will be between fundamentalists of both groups, and between the liberals.

Yes. It will be the fundamentalists, Catholics and Protestants, who will join forces. The Roman Catholics always give the appearance of desperately wanting unity. On the local level they will cooperate in ecumenical services, but later they will rebaptize or otherwise give little consideration to those "outside Rome." While demanding non-Roman baptismal certificates, they present the pope's visit to the United States as a call for unity. But the call is a call for a return to Rome. It is the Protestants who are more apt to continue doing radical things to prove the spirit of unity. Holding the 1979 consecration of Episcopal Bishop Arthur Walmsley of Connecticut in Saint Joseph's Roman Catholic Cathedral is an example. Making a rabbi a canon of the Cathedral of Saint John the Divine is another. This is merely unity for appearance. God is God to these churches, but their organizational and doctrinal beliefs are polarized. Efforts toward unity can effect a coming together of spirit, but one "super-church" will never be workable unless each group is willing to relinquish much of its history and teaching.

3. The church will interest only those people whose "psychological age" is about 45 years and older.

Actual interest in and loyalty to churches on the part of people in this age group is evident in the yearly church conventions and in weekly church attendance. Commitment to Jesus Christ for younger Christians today does not imply a denomination or a building. And efforts to hold youth by "activities" will no longer be successful. Church researcher, Dr. Merton Strommen, president of Search Institute of Minneapolis, Minnesota, commenting on the failure of youth ministries and decline of youth in the institutional churches during the 1960s and 1970s, said it was the church's "failure to take seriously the spiritual growth needs of youth as they were being challenged to solve social problems . . . there was little emphasis on prayer, bible study, and personal commitment to Christ." The recent Gallup poll revealed that 95 percent of American teenagers believe in God or in a "Universal Spirit"; three out of four of them believe in a "personal" God. They say that they pray and that they have strong religious inclinations. But they are not filling today's churches, nor, in my opinion, will they fill tomorrow's churches.

4. Total church membership will decrease, but those remaining will be knowledgeable and more committed.

Dr. Tapp believes that as time goes on fewer youth will be interested in joining churches. This does not mean, however, that they will not learn more about how to cope with life at all levels. New approaches such as "possibility thinking," "mind training," and "ways to mental and spiritual health" will be substituted for the teaching of the church. New developments in scientific thought will also be acceptable to youth. Such developments may effect a kind of science-religion-philosophy merger that will be the basis of a "Cosmic Christ" approach to the future for these young people. Interestingly enough, Dr. Tapp thinks that the cutoff age of interest in the formal churches will no longer be at the high school level, but at the junior high age.

The people who do remain in the conventional churches will be willing to devote more time to the study of the church's doctrines and tradition. They will consider themselves custodians of the faith, and, thus, there will always be a remnant who will know what the Christian religion is all about. In the long run (even beyond the year 2000) this will strengthen the church. Even if there must be an underground church, the members of that church will more truly and faithfully represent historical Christianity.

5. More people (not all necessarily Christians) will believe that the Christian's primary concern should be with some form of social action.

Certainly, as Dr. Tapp demonstrated in his report, Christians have turned to service of others without regard to religious views of those in need. The modern Christian is not a person obsessed with personal salvation. In recent times his philosophy as well as his theology has been concerned with "putting the world straight." This may continue for some time, in my view, but with the rise of charismatic religion and the new emphasis on fundamentalism, it is not difficult to surmise that the religious trend will move again in the direction of an emphasis on personal salvation. Rightly so. But not in the vein of the "born again" demands of the old-time religion. What will be needed, as the frenzy in the church is reduced, is an updated and sensible understanding of the ancient doctrine of individual salvation.

6. Most church school teachers will see their function as "fellow seekers" with their students.

I have known this to be true recently, and I think that it is not a wrong approach at all since we are all on the road to the Ultimate. But rather than training themselves in the history and theology of the Christian faith, many present-day church-school teachers seem to be attempting merely to be one step ahead. The Christian churches must be in a state of constant revision of their study materials. The idea of Sunday school now seems to have passed its peak and it is difficult to project large-scale educational programs for youth. The new program called "Shared Approaches," which has been developed and approved by a dozen different denominations for use at all levels of their educational efforts, is now available and in use. But it has not yet been tested enough to provide any way to make an adequate evaluation of its usefulness. Whether, in this joint effort, the churches have demanded of themselves a high enough standard is yet to be seen.

7. The Consultation on Church Union proposals will be adopted.

Dr. Tapp thinks that this may still happen, but it certainly will not be without its problems. Such a united church will be larger but not necessarily individualistic. And it may require some abandonment of doctrines once held essential. Such doctrines will recede into the church's historical memory and will be retained only in restructured form in the new worship services. Hints of this may already be observed in the more liberal approach to the service of Holy Communion and the entire doctrine of the Sacraments.

8. There will be no more single denominational Christian educational programs.

I have already mentioned the new "Shared Approaches" program that has been devised and adopted by at least twelve national churches. There are also half a dozen or so independent producers of religious educational material whose courses are being chosen by individual churches. Yet there is already evidence of unhappiness with any kind of packaged approach to religious education. This is especially true when such packages are prepared by one of the "nameless, faceless bureaucracies" in New York, Nashville, or St. Louis.

> 9. There will be no more support for the building of massive church "plants" such as were built in the 50's and 60's.

One of the main reasons for the lack of interest in huge new sanctuaries and educational buildings is that decreased attendance at formal church functions will make it impossible to support financially such buildings. To be sure, the flashy new structures that will appear are those built by the television and radio preachers who want monuments to themselves. Church building sponsored and backed financially by denominational headquarters is already in a noticeable decline. The great structures such as the Cathedral of Saint John the Divine in New York City and the National Cathedral in Washington may be the last of the churches in the grand tradition.

> 10. Integration of all minorities will become a fact within the churches.

This has already taken place at all levels—and rightly so. There are still diehards who object, but integration is now an established fact. People have learned that when it comes to the spiritual life, each of us is seeking and must be allowed to seek side by side.

> 11. The churches will give up their tax-exempt status.

Although this has not yet happened nationally, it is evident that if the churches paid even a 4 or 5 percent tax, such an amount would be of great significance to the benefit of the country. The most conservative estimate of the amount of property owned by the church bodies of the United States places its value in excess of $80 billion. This fact is bringing an increasing number of calls for the church to pay its way in our society. Perhaps even earlier than the year 2000 churches will no longer enjoy such a privilege.

12. Foreign missions will be less emphasized and will probably be replaced by some kind of Peace Corps-type activity.

What was once considered mission—reaching the heathen with the Gospel in an effort to convert them to Christianity—has changed. Mission now falls more under the category of service to others than attempts to convert them. Dr. Tapp believes that by the year 2000 "anything that smacks of full-time evangelistic efforts will neither be supported at home nor tolerated abroad." Already many Third World countries are refusing to accept Christian evangelists.

13. Lay academies will increase in number and in influence among Christian denominations.

Churches will be more insistent that individuals have competent training in order to teach in church schools and study groups. No longer will lay people be allowed to inflict their personal philosophies and theologies and prejudices on children and new converts. There will be a high standard set for teaching in the church. Moreover, such teaching will require a solid knowledge of good psychology and the social sciences as well as church history and theology. Schools of religion will have to be sponsored by the various denominations, as they are now, in order to protect their own historical background; but such schools will have to be linked with the major secular universities in order to insure that their students do not receive an isolated and provincial education.

14. Denominational theological seminaries will not be able to operate without reference to university-level education.

This is almost a corollary of the point listed immediately above. But it applies more particularly to the professional training schools for future priests and ministers. Since the denominational seminaries will find it more and more difficult to survive financially, they will be forced to join with graduate schools of other disciplines in order to remain alive. In doing this, they will necessarily relinquish what have previously been the distinguishing marks of their denominational affiliation. Some seminaries will find it possible to merge with others; others will perish. Moreover, a considerable number of students in seminaries will not be aiming at ordination for the ministry but will be pursuing their own religious quest without regard to achieving competence in the traditional courses required by denominational authorities. Of course, this means that more and more women will be found in seminaries. All of the mainline theological schools will experience a rising tide of educated women; the Roman Catholic church, especially, will be forced to deal with the demand for ordained women priests.

15. Theology will move toward an emphasis on panentheism and away from the traditional interest in transcendence and immanence.

Panentheism holds that God is *in* everything (as contrasted with pantheism, which is the doctrine that God *is* everything); that is, more and more people are going to view the universe and all that is in it as manifesting God. This is considerably different from the traditional belief that God is "above" the world and distinct from it, or that he is "with" the world as an in-dwelling Spirit. Dr. Tapp sees the new emphasis as a return to an ancient view of the world, which is becoming more and more appealing to a scientifically oriented society that is reexamining the thought forms of the Eastern religions. Certainly we have already seen the impact of Eastern thought on our younger generation and in the influx of every conceivable kind of psychic, astrological, and metaphysical approach to reality. One can easily agree with Dr. Tapp that in a scientifically trained population the challenge to the church is enormous.

16. The national Boards and Agencies of the major denominations will merge, coalesce, and generally lose their authority and influence.

Although this point was specifically related to his own church, Dr. Tapp sees these mergers as occurring not only because of the loss of sufficient funds to maintain their enormous structures, but also because of the increasing necessity for the development of some kind of "think tank" for the whole Christian enterprise in this country. It may be that each major denomination will require such a think tank to set the pace and chart the course for its total outreach. But such a group will not be charged with implementing programs; both authority and responsibility for action will be returned to the local level. And, of course, some way must be devised to keep the local churches from becoming entities unto themselves if any Christian historical tradition is to endure.

17. Sermons are out. And so is the traditional Sunday morning worship service.

When any kind of prediction like this one is made, the immediate reaction is to say that it is impossibly radical. But it may not be impossible. Bad sermons, casual and haphazard worship practices, inappropriate and badly performed music, and a continuing failure to truly encounter the mystery of the sacred—all have contributed to the increasing loss of interest in the conventional Sunday morning worship service. If this continues, the church of the future will be so separated from the mainstream of American life that it will be considered only as a harmless and innocuous pastime for elderly citizens.

I do not want to be misunderstood. This does not mean that the life and teaching of Jesus Christ will become less meaningful. It does not mean that the essence of worship will be forever lost. It does mean that, given the above conditions, worship will not be like worship as we know it now. But worship is an essential element in the human personality; in one form or another, we shall have it in the year 2000.

18. College students and young adults will show increasing interest in religion, including Christianity—but not institutional Christianity.

This has already taken place even if it has not always been readily acknowledged by the officials of institutional Christianity. As we have seen in our discussion of the cults and the Charismatics, our youth have turned in great numbers to the gurus and holy men, to strange doctrines and even witchcraft. Dr. Tapp believes that young people will continue to avoid the institutional church. Believing will not necessarily be belonging. The institutional church has simply not met the needs of young people in their relentless search for both knowledge and experience in the realms of religion; they will not settle for anything less than the best in the years ahead.

19. The appeal to "fellowship" will no longer be enough to attract people to the activities of local churches.

True. All of the frantically conceived devices designed to bring people into a shallow circle of contrived "fellowship" have already lost whatever effectiveness they once had. Moreover, such a kind and degree of fellowship is not needed. People have a much greater choice of places to go and things to do than they have ever had before. The church is no longer the center of social life in the community. And, in the midst of an already overstrenuous life, people need the quietness of a protected life at home. Especially for those people who work in crowded offices in big cities, who commute to work on jammed buses and subway trains, the thought of going out again at night for an evening of "fellowship" at the church is simply nonsense. They do not want it and they do not need it. Does this mean, then, that such group activities as the church offers will be accepted only by those people who cannot cope with the demands of ordinary social and business life? When the church speaks of "fellowship," does it mean a fellowship of the emotionally crippled, the dropouts and rejects of society? If so, what does the tradition-hallowed phrase "the community of believers" mean for the church of the year 2000?

20. There will be less interest in separate men's and women's programs. And some people will belong to more than one church.

As we have evolved a "unisex" society, such a society has appeared in our churches. Things will be done together in the church of the future—whether it be membership on official boards, in the various service organizations of the church, or as delegates to regional and national conventions of the denomination. Church members will participate in the affairs of their churches as church members, not as men or women. Men's clubs are already nearly extinct, and women's organizations are rapidly growing weaker.

21. Television will be used as a major educational tool by clusters of churches across the country. By such means, the very best church school teachers can be brought to any church, large or small.

In the future every effort will have to be made to utilize the best of technical resources at every point in the educational program of the church. We are just at the beginning of a major breakthrough in our knowledge and techniques of the learning process. The church simply cannot allow itself to fall behind; to do so is to fail its own biblical directives. The problem today is that most priests, pastors, and church educators are already so far behind that it is almost impossible for them to catch up.

22. The breakdown of authority will continue to spread; that is, the authority of the Bible, of pastors, of vestry, session, or other official bodies, within the structure of the church has all but disappeared. As the years go by, this breakdown will continue.

In the eleven years since 1969, this loss of authority has been almost complete. People not only do not know where authority resides, they do not even care. And this means that attempts to reconstitute ecclesiastical and doctrinal authority are doomed to failure. Does it also mean that those who have been ordained to represent authority have abandoned their own self-convictions as to their roles in the Christian community?

23. The church stands in very great danger of losing the intellectual elite of this country.

This is already happening, and at an ever-increasing rate. And it is happening to both clergy and laity ranks in the church. The local clergyman was once considered to be the most educated man in the community. He was the scholar, the classicist, the informed person on all matters of interest to his people. Not so today. In many cases, the clergyman is a poor example of the value of education; in some instances, the best that one can say is that he is a buffoon. He is now merely a people pleaser.

But it has not always been so in this country. In *The Power of Their Glory: The Episcopalians,* by Kit and Frederica Konolige, the influence of the people and the priests of the Episcopalian church is examined. The Rev. Roger Hamilton, in a review of this book, says that the Episcopalian church "is the direct result of the involvement of people of means in the life of the church. It is the story of an era which has passed that had sophisticated, affable people, it had simplicity and good taste, it [the book] is the story of the people who made, in large part, for good or ill, our country and our church what it is today."

But perhaps the most far-reaching effect on the church is the loss of the people whom sociologist Peter Berger calls "the cognitive minority," the men and women who are the best educated, the most perceptive, the most influential—these are the people who are no longer interested in the kind of petty games that most churches today seem to be playing. Without such people, the church rapidly fades into mediocrity as an influence in the lives of individual men and women and in society as a whole. Who, any longer, first asks the church what it thinks before major national and international decisions are taken?

24. The present resurgence of interest in formal worship is only momentary.

To my way of thinking, all of the special efforts to update the ritual and modernize worship are temporary. Such efforts will not be the means by which the church can revitalize itself. Since 1969 we have noted the supreme effort that has been made to continue the kind of contemporary "additions" to worship that were so popular in the 1950s and early 1960s. And a good number of pastors and priests still think that such "contemporary" approaches to worship are needed in order to attract people to the church and the Christian life. They will not. Nor will they sustain the faithful who remain.

Ritual making is not the answer. Americans, to be sure, are noted for concocting one new fad after another. And so we have treated the ancient rituals of Christianity as if they were aging TV productions whose initial success has begun to fade so that what is now needed to restore the bloom is simply a new "angle" or a new "format." This is what we are now doing. If we continue to follow such fads in worship, the church beyond the year 2000 will not be recognizable.

25. The church of A.D. 2000 will not be recognizable by anyone who knows it today.

Dr. Tapp thinks that the church of the future may well be like some kind of "futuristic Qumran." In other words, he sees the church turning in on itself. And when it does it will eventually be unable to recognize itself as a Christian community of faith. The church will have lost its zest for living. Or else the vitality of the Holy Spirit that has kept the church alive for twenty centuries will cause it to reappear in forms almost entirely different from anything we have known before.

Martin E. Marty, in 1969, felt that the church was in the midst of a trend toward the secular and that a "new style of consciousness, sensibility, and social organization" was on the horizon. "Something institutional will survive," he said, "but it will be transformed." Marcus Bach wrote that denominationalism would become obsolete and that "Church Street, 2001, will be a place where individuals turn more and more to mystical explorations, recognizing a greater affinity with the universe and dealing more with the unseen than the seen. It will be a way of life and everyone's experience with the unseen and the seen will be a natural part of it . . ."

Billy Graham, in a 1979 talk to clergy in Canada, reminded them that the projections for the world ahead are so staggering that it is almost inconceivable how the clergy will be able to minister to what is envisioned for the future. And Hiley Ward, in his book *Religion 2101,* presents a truly mind-boggling list of projections for religious patterns.

I would like to suggest a further challenge to the church that may well increase its present frenzy. And I do so knowing that the projection might result in some loss of reader credibility of this writing. It is the now-controversial subject of the Unidentified Flying Objects. Are they the next major theological challenge? This query was, indeed, the subject of an article in the February 22, 1978 issue of *The Christian Century.*

The rise of interest in UFO's has been steadily increasing for many years. It was further encouraged by the production of the film *Close Encounters of the Third Kind* and several recent television series. There is now available a vast amount of literature on the subject. The Edmund Scientific Company, in Barrington, New Jersey, offers numerous filmstrips and tape commentaries to the interested student. The tape recordings feature Dr. J. Allen Hynek of Northwestern University. Dr. Hynek established a Center for UFO Studies at 924 Chicago Avenue, Evanston, Illinois. He is now considered the top expert in the world, having collected and investigated reports of these phenomena for many years. The center now has a "hot line" with an "800" telephone number available to police, planetariums, and certain federal offices.

I met Professor Hynek a few years ago in a special meeting attended also by astronaut Edgar Mitchell. It was an evening I shall never forget. The range of conversation went far beyond everyday ideas and orthodox science. Dr. Hynek firmly believes that within his lifetime we shall have arrived at the proof necessary to establish beyond doubt that we are not alone in the universe. And eventually, even the ordinary citizen will have to deal with more than mere speculative fiction about the relation between some aspects of science and religion. The future will bring with it a new era of theological debate. And those new struggles that face theology will surely dwarf to insignificance such issues as women clergy and new liturgies.

The coming theological debate will be so profound that it will create new mysteries about our place in the scheme of things. I have no doubt that only through complete faith in God as Creator and Sustainer of the entire universe will we be able to survive such challenges. This also means that we may find ourselves facing a new understanding of what it means to say that "Jesus Christ is the same, now and forever." In what ways will we come to know that his divine life reaffirms the nature of God and the true calling of mankind?

In the *Christian Century* article referred to above, there is a quotation from Frederic Brussat with which I thoroughly agree: "Christians will never be able to live down the shortsightedness of the medieval churchmen who refused to peer through Galileo's telescope. They were not willing to deal with more than one world. And they were afraid to take seriously the implications of a powerful new way of looking at reality. It would be a grave error and an irresponsible act for religious people of our time to ignore the myth of the extraterrestrial or to try to reason UFO's out of existence."

Life calls for many adjustments. What were once fears are now matters of faith and practice. As Christians, we must always look to the future with positive thoughts. If there is life elsewhere in the universe then whatever their belief we will have to deal with it in the context of our own faith and in the light of what the Master has taught us. We should then be able to apply goodness, love, and faith to any aspect of

God's universe. Thus there is much to learn in the years ahead, and the challenge is not very far ahead. It is here with us now—speaking through a church in frenzy.

In *The Last Years of the Church* David Poling says:

The concentration on the church as a place, a geographic location, is not enough to shape a powerful and meaningful witness to the world. Whether we search the Scriptures or examine the exhortations of the saints for guidance, the body of Christ is primarily a fellowship called out of the world on one hand, and, on the other, sent into the world to witness to the Name.[1]

Arthur Herzog, in *The Church Trap,* says:

The noticeable drift in modern religion away from traditional structure and belief has brought with it problems not just in identity, but in maintaining the institutional church. Catholics may well wonder, as they abandon symbol after symbol, why they call themselves by that name, and Protestants why they belong to a church at all. Indeed, warns Paul Ramsey, the Protestant theologian, the church is becoming a "secular sect" and the desire to tell the secular world how to handle its troubles is a fig leaf to cover the unseemly parts of a disintegrated Christian understanding.[2]

In *Where Have All Our People Gone?* Carl S. Dudley writes:

The evidence of declining membership is indisputable, but the causes for lost membership are not as clear, since there is no single path by which we can trace the departure. These lost members have not trooped off en masse to join other denominations or religious groups and they do not seem to be angry with the church as such. Without defining all the causes, we can identify a massive shift of cultural values during the 1960's. The largest number of lost members is associated with the rising religious affirmation of New Believers.[3]

In the October 1977 issue of *The Futurist* there are forty-one problems listed that we must eventually face. They were identified by researchers at Stanford Research Institute's International Center for the Study of Social Policy. Among them are the effects of stress on individuals and on society, the misuse of consciousness technologies and psychic abilities, catastrophic experiments, computer dependency (including advanced microcomputers), rights to privacy, and the effects of technology on the individual psyche. These and other problems in the world ahead pose issues for the church as it evolves new pastoral techniques and approaches to an understanding of the Gospel in what can only be called "Future Church." And these are the issues that are causing, right now, what *The Futurist* calls an "increasing dependence of the individual on technology for the satisfaction of his needs."

If clergy crack up in the midst of increasing pressures of society and a changing world, then it is because they have not been able to cope with the emerging trends. Dr. Samuel Blizzard, the Princeton sociologist, studied 690 clergymen. He examined two things: "the role that lay people expect of their ministers and the role that ministers expect of themselves." His conclusion: "The new American culture has resulted in a change in what people expect of the minister. In the past, the parish clergyman performed his function as a general practitioner. Now he is expected to be a specialist." Pastor LeMar Clark of Detroit commented: "And he is expected to be a specialist in not one or two but in six or seven separate roles: preacher, administrator, organizer, pastor, priest, and teacher." Clark continued: "The tensions between congregations and their ministers, arising out of today's impossible ministerial role, are not going to be resolved without

honest appraisal on the part of the clergy and cooperative
effort on the part of the lay people." He might well have
added the warning . . . "else the frenzy in the church will
widen and deepen."

Lay people still have their own frustrations with the
church in frenzy today. They are not thinking of the future.
They are thinking of now, now, now! Layman Robert B.
Feild, whose deceased father was a priest, wrote his bishop a
letter. It concerned a lecture on the revered Episcopal Book
of Common Prayer given by a seminary professor. Feild referred to the professor's talk of "degenerate evangelistic pie-
tism and degenerate Roman piety." The professor had said:
"The new Book of Common Prayer has recovered the nature
of the Holy Spirit." But Feild observed: "I resent being told
that I had lost the Holy Spirit. I am sure that I never have
and never will comprehend the Holy Spirit, but I did get
some glimmering through the old Book. That Professor described the Three Hour Service on Good Friday as being
something more like a Peruvian Roman Catholic than an
Episcopalian service. Well, there are a lot of Peruvian Roman Catholics in the Protestant Episcopal Church in the
USA, is all I can say!" And Robert Feild represents a vast
segment of what may or may not be a future church—even
half a dozen years from now.

Whether we like it or not, we are entering an ecumenical age. Diversity is only the beginning, and brainstorming is
the mechanical technique of making it happen. The Holy
Spirit can only too easily become the excuse for making it
happen.

There are two kinds of prophecy. One tells us of the
situation as it really is. The other speaks of what may be the
result of the present situation. Some prophets view trends as
a prelude to the future. Other prophets view what they see as
permission to say that "all's well"—and to urge us to go onward and upward to new and glorious success . . . whether
that onward and upward has any relation to reality or not.

As an example of what is surely going on in all of the mainline denominations, here is an excerpt from a sermon delivered by the dean of Trinity Cathedral, Trenton, New Jersey. He said:

> One of the most important lessons which many of us should learn from the experience of the most recent General Convention of our church is that what we had been led to believe about our Episcopal Church and its future just isn't so. We all know that the Episcopal Church has been going through a most traumatic period in her history since the special convention in South Bend ten years ago. The social upheavals of the sixties, liturgical renewal, women in Holy Orders, and the proposed but soundly defeated attempt to permit the ordination of homosexual persons, were all used by the church's detractors and those of uncertain faith to predict the rapid demise of the American branch of the Anglican Communion.
>
> Our secular pollsters told us how many people we had lost and predicted that by the year 2000 there would be one priest for each surviving communicant. And the tragedy is that so many believed the prophets of doom. The Denver General Convention assured me that what so many believed so firmly really isn't so. And, in making this discovery about herself, the Episcopal Church has found the key to her future life and progress. Indeed, one of our church's most critical self-evaluating publications conceded at Denver that the Episcopal Church has probably never been in better shape than she is today.

That statement may be the actual belief of the dean or it may be a subconscious wish to heal and to persuade a congregation to go on being loyal. Nevertheless, the fact of the matter is that the Episcopal church is not in the best of shape but is more fragmented than ever. And the same thing is true of the two major Presbyterian denominations, the United Methodists and the Lutherans.

Hope is surely a central theme in Christianity and in the history of the church. The hope that was given in the drama of the Resurrection is the sustaining power of Christ himself. That hope will never be dimmed. But that is not really the question for us.

Every living institution must undergo necessary change and adaptation. But this does not mean throwing away centuries of tradition for today's latest fad. All too often, the mainline churches have undercut their own foundations by desperately trying to be "with it" and in the process succeeded only in confusing and alienating those they so desperately wish to serve.

Whether or not the institutional church is to survive is really the question. We must not think, however, of the church only as we know it. Future church may well be unlike anything we can imagine at this moment. Until then, we have only the present church structures with which to work and in which to live and serve. Should we not make them as respectable and inwardly palatable as possible? Should we not look to our tradition to give us guidance into the future?

FOOTNOTES

CHAPTER ONE

1. Jackson W. Carroll, Douglas W. Johnson, and Martin E. Marty, *Religion in America: 1950 to the Present* (New York: Harper & Row, Publishers, 1979), pp. 113–15.

CHAPTER TWO

1. Paul Seabury, "Trendier Than Thou," *Harper's,* October 1978, pp. 39–52.
2. Michael Manley, "The Shackles of Domination and Oppression," *The Witness,* Spring 1976, pp. 9–11.
3. James E. Griffiss, "The Anglican Experience of Authority" (Address printed by The Diocese of New Jersey, January 18, 1978).

CHAPTER THREE

1. James Gardner Hodder, "Christianity and Sex," *The Christian Challenge,* October 1970, pp. 18–19.
2. Bennett J. Sims, "Sex and Homosexuality," *Christianity Today,* February 24, 1978, pp. 23–30.
3. Mary Strong, *Letters of The Scattered Brotherhood* (New York: Harper & Row, Publishers, 1948), p. 57.

4. Walter Wink, "Biblical Perspectives on Homosexuality," *The Christian Century,* November 7, 1979, pp. 1082–86.

CHAPTER FOUR

1. "Pentecostalism 'Real Threat' to Church Integrity," *The Living Church,* September 23, 1973.
2. Preliminary Report, The Study Commission on Glossalia, Division of Pastoral Services, The Episcopal Diocese of California, Rev. David Forbes, Chairman. Submitted to the Bishop, May 2, 1963; released May 14, 1963. Cf. "Pastoral Letter" required by the Ordinary to be read in all Churches of the Diocese at all morning services on the Third Sunday after Easter, 1963. Signed by James A. Pike, Bishop of California.

CHAPTER FIVE

1. Louis Cassels, *What's the Difference?*
2. Carroll E. Simcox, *Death By a Thousand Cuts.* (Eureka Springs, Ark.: The Fellowship of Concerned Churchmen, n.d.), p. 7.

CHAPTER SIX

1. Harvey Cox, "Why Young Americans Are Buying Oriental Religions," *Psychology Today,* July 1977, pp. 36–42.

CHAPTER SEVEN

1. David Poling, *The Last Years of the Church* (Old Tappan, N. J.: Fleming H. Revell Company, 1969), p. 131.
2. Arthur Herzog, *The Church Trap* (New York: The Macmillan Company, 1968), p. 167.
3. Carl S. Dudley, *Where Have All Our People Gone?* (New York: The Pilgrim Press, 1979), p. 115.